# Israel
# and the
# Politics of Land

W Eugen March
12/12/96

# Israel
# and the
# Politics of Land

## A Theological
## Case Study

W. Eugene March

Westminster/John Knox Press
Louisville, Kentucky

Scripture quotations from the New Revised Standard Version of the Bible are copyright © 1989 by the Division of Christian Education of the National Council of the Churches of Christ in the U.S.A., and are used by permission.

*Book design by Susan E. Jackson*

*Cover design by Drew Stevens*

*First edition*

Published by Westminster/John Knox Press
Louisville, Kentucky

This book is printed on acid-free paper that meets the American National Standards Institute Z39.48 standard. ∞

PRINTED IN THE UNITED STATES OF AMERICA

9 8 7 6 5 4 3 2 1

**Library of Congress Cataloging-in-Publication Data**

March, W. Eugene (Wallace Eugene), date.
    Israel and the politics of land : a theological case study / W. Eugene March. — 1st ed.
        p.    cm.
    Includes bibliographical references.
    ISBN 0-664-25121-8 (alk. paper)
    1. Jewish-Arab relations—Religious aspects.    2. Palestine in the Bible.    3. Bible. O.T.—Criticism, interpretation, etc.    4. palestine in Judaism.    5. Palestine in Christianity.    6. Land tenure—Religious aspects.    I. Title.
DS119.7.M293    1994
231.7'6—dc20                     93-40125

# Contents

Foreword        vii

Preface        xi

1. People and Land:
   Many Faces, Many Voices      1

2. The Realities of History:      17
   People, Power, and Palestine

3. God and Earth-keeping:      45
   Biblical Perspectives on Land

4. God's Way and Israel:      65
   Theological Reflections on a Particular Land

5. A Guiding Vision:      83
   A Call to Be Earth-keepers

Group Study Guide      99

# Foreword

W. Eugene March has spent a long, distinguished career thinking carefully and with discernment as a Reformed theologian about the land of the Middle East, and now this book presents his mature and judicious judgment. At the same time that this book summarizes his long years of scholarly reflection, it also exhibits his serious church engagement in the issue of Jewish-Palestinian relations, as he has contributed crucially to the thought and policy of the Presbyterian Church (U.S.A.) on the question.

March's thoughtful book in a quite distinctive way concerns the difficult linkage between biblical faith and practical political reality. That linkage has not often been taken up critically. On the one hand, there are rich and suggestive studies on the "land theme" in the Bible, but they characteristically stop before they get to the hard part, contemporary issues of land in the Holy Land. On the other hand, much contemporary opinion about the politics of the Holy Land is expansively influenced by romantic religion, facile propaganda, or profound cynicism.

March weaves his way through these reductionist alternatives in characteristically understated but enormously courageous ways. His primary *critical* contribution is to insist that the contemporary state of Israel must be radically separated from all "biblical claims to the land," the sorts of claims enunciated by the state of Israel itself, and by some "Christian friends" of the state of Israel. Thus, says March: "Israel is not biblical Israel"; "It is not right to say modern Israel is chosen by God in some way other nations are not"; "Israelis do not have divine right to any land. . . ." This is a daring and exceedingly important critical conclusion.

But March is not finished at that point, which is essentially negative concerning the self-presentation of the state of Israel. March takes the next crucial step, which is imperative for a Reformed theologian, by making a powerful *constructive* statement. On the one hand, realism mandates that Israel, like every nation–state, is entitled to secure boundaries and legitimacy that make identity and survival possible. On the other hand, Israel, like every nation–state, exists in a world where God the Creator governs. God as Creator means that there is a moral fabric to international politics to which every nation–state is summoned and by which every nation–state finally is assessed. Moreover, this Creator God works and wills well-being for nation–states, as they operate responsibly in their proper zone, and attends to their pertinent "neighbor questions."

While this book tackles the vexing issue of the state of Israel, March has articulated a very large theory of politics, whereby all nations (including Israel, but also including the United States) are subject to a genuine "other" beyond themselves by whom much is required and much is given. This way of thinking has a kind of depth and seriousness that romantic "biblical" attitudes toward Israel do not even approximate.

This book will not please zealots. It will not please advocates of the Palestinians who want to deny Israel its political legitimacy. It will not please partisans of Israel who want biblical warrants for Israel's identity. It will not please religious romantics who tie the future of Israel to messianic claims.

March did not set out to please. Instead, his intent is to show that thinking theologically in the Reformed tradition inescapably bears upon lived reality in the public domain. The book, like all March's work, is subtle and quiet. His mode of understatement, however, does not detract from the evident success and enormous contribution of the work. I am pleased to celebrate the work of my longtime friend and respected colleague, as he makes a case that will now become the base line for all serious theological thinking on these complex issues. The book is powerfully compelling and methodologically subtle. It will require careful reading and give reward commensurate to such care.

Walter Brueggemann
Columbia Theological Seminary
May 4, 1993

# Preface

This book primarily is about land and how we think about it. It is written from a Reformed Christian perspective, which means at the least that the Bible is an important underpinning and that the transformation of human society is an acknowledged goal. Reformation and reconciliation are important to Reformed Christians. Justice is a standard we hold especially high. Compassion is the mode of justice.

The thesis of this book is that land is best understood as a divine loan intended for responsible (righteous and just) use. Human communities require land, but they can never claim full ownership and are ever to be judged by how they exercise dominion over the land. The biblical account concerning ancient Israel is the primary basis for this thesis. The Bible presents standards by which to measure conflicting claims about and uses of land in this one world we all inhabit.

As a means of sharpening theological insight about land, I concentrate here upon a specific piece of land that has been of interest to many different people for many centuries. This land is located at the eastern end of the Mediterranean Sea and serves as a bridge between Africa and Asia. The earliest biblical sources call this bridge the "land of Canaan." The Romans named it "Palestine." For more than four thousand years, armies have marched back and forth through this area as various nations have sought domination. A better understanding of the history and significance of this land and its people is an additional goal of this study.

The land in question is now known as Israel. Israel is a small country; more than half of its population is concentrated in the coastal plain, a narrow band of arable land about 170 miles long from north to south and about 10 to 25 miles wide. The interior of the land is hilly and rocky. The eastern side of the land is marked by the Jordan Valley, and to the south lies the Negev Desert. From the extreme northern point to the southernmost point is 260 miles, and from east to west the distance at the widest is 72 miles. If the territory that Israel has occupied since 1967 is included, the country is about the size of Maryland.

The attention that Israel receives far exceeds its size, resources, or strategic location (which is not nearly as significant in our modern world as it was in antiquity). The creation of the modern Israel on land once occupied by the biblical Israelites is one major reason for the scrutiny. Some see this as the fulfillment of ancient prophecy. Others see it as part of an imperialist plot. Still others see Israel as a haven for Jews in a world where the hatred of Jews is still rampant. Jews, Christians, and Muslims all claim a special relationship with the place, a fact that heightens sensitivities all the more.

The level of interest that Israel and the Middle East command was made dramatically clear in late 1993 when, for the first time in decades, the possibility of actual peace seemed to emerge. Israel and the Palestinians, along with some of the neighboring Arab states, moved toward defining a new relationship among themselves. Central to that relationship was the mutual recognition of the several parties and a commitment to work toward a resolution of the vast differences that have separated Israel and the Palestinians. The plan aims at assuring limited self-rule in the Gaza Strip and in Jericho in exchange for a recognition of Israel's right to exist and a guarantee of secure borders. This new relationship, though of momentous importance, has not yet led to a detailed plan which can assure peace in the area. The ultimate resolution of the land issues lies years in the future, possibly in the new century. Nonetheless, this was a significant move and will affect the way the parties involved view and deal with the land.

While one of my goals is to enable readers, especially North American Christians, to become better informed about the history and significance of modern Israel, I also have a wider objective, namely an understanding and appreciation of God's claim on all land. The search for a just peace in the Middle East involves knowledge about the peculiar history of the peoples of the area. But the principles that guide the search can be applied to any conflict over land—whether in the Middle East, Central America, the United States, or wherever.

Central to any effort to work toward reformation and reconciliation is the conviction that God alone is Creator and Adjudicator. God has created the world and appointed human beings as "earth-keepers." We are all held accountable in accordance with this divine appointment. It is hoped that reflection about a particular place, Israel, may help us to understand more concretely the possibilities, both positive and negative, of exercising dominion over any land. The wider goal is to recognize and work toward faithfully fulfilling our God-given roles as "earth-keepers" wherever we live.

This book is intended as a contribution toward understanding the significance of land, God's land, and to its just and righteous use. If I have incorrectly interpreted the views of others, they are honest mistakes, not malicious distortions. It is certainly my hope that any misunderstandings can be corrected and that they will not stand in the way of the wider views of this book. As "earth-keepers" we are obligated to right injustices and to secure peace wherever possible. Such a mandate requires that we get on with the task.

# 1 | People and Land: Many Faces, Many Voices

This book about land begins with the people who live on the land. This beginning point is chosen for several reasons. First, the people of Israel are fascinating in their multiplicity and diversity. Many who have never visited Israel are amazed by the wide variety of people who live within this small country. Israel is in some ways a microcosm of our world, with many ethnic, language, racial, and religious communities. The reality of Israel quickly challenges and shatters many stereotypes. This is a surprise to many.

Second, many of the people in Israel hold strong views about the land. Often, they have a greater attachment to land than is usually expressed by urbanites in Europe or the United States. Many people in Israel are prepared to fight and even die for the land. To begin to understand these people is to gain insight into how questions about the land might be framed and addressed. To ignore the people living on the land so central to the biblical accounts would surely be a mistake.

Third, the people who live on the land express several contrasting views about the land. If anyone were tempted to believe there is a single Jewish position or a single Arab understanding or a single Christian teaching, speaking with the people who live within Israel will at least give serious cause for hesitancy. Before a view is fashioned about the theological significance of land, it is important to listen to and reflect upon what real people have to say about the crucial topic. Israel's pluralism is critical to recognize and hear.

1

Finally, to start with the people is to acknowledge the centuries-long struggles provoked by claims about and over land. To talk about land in the abstract would surely be a disservice. Land takes on significance because it is claimed, tilled, built upon, treasured, and loved by human beings. The passions and controversies encountered in Israel are reflections of similar feelings and commitments around the globe. Any theological reflection about land needs to be informed by the reality of the conflicts, the injustices, and the vision that land evokes in that particular space. Some believe that the only solution is to quit talking about land altogether and stress the oneness and unity of humankind. The reality of Israel, however, argues not for less reflection and talk about land, but for more. Thus, the people of Israel—for whom the debate over land is vigorous—offer an appropriate beginning place for the discussion.

## The Setting

Israel is a parliamentary democracy, and its multiparty political system reflects the cultural, ethnic, and ideological diversity of Israel's population. The openness and freedom of its debates are uncommon in most of the Middle East. A multiplicity of opinions about almost every significant issue is readily apparent in Israel and is considered a national value.

By history and tradition, Jerusalem is the preeminent city in Israel. Its population of approximately 490,000 reflects the cultural, ethnic, religious, and political diversity of the country more clearly than any other city or region. Israel declared Jerusalem its capital in 1980, an action still disputed by many governments around the world. At the center of this modern city is a very old section known as the Old City. Surrounded by a wall about two and a half miles long built in 1537 C.E. by the Ottoman ruler, Sultan Suleiman the Magnificent, the Old City peculiarly exemplifies the cultural and religious diversity of contemporary Israel. For many centuries, Muslims, Christians, and Jews have occupied parts of this town. Sometimes one group banned others, but each group was always aware of the others and the claims of tradition that each group had on this place.

Some of the most ancient remains of biblical Jerusalem have been uncovered within the Old City, and some of the most modern tensions are being lived out here. The people who go in and out of the Old City offer a microcosm of Israeli society. Spending time at two historic gates into the Old City, Damascus Gate and Jaffa Gate, provides a dramatic illustration of the diversity of Israel's population and the multiplicity of views about land.

## The People of Damascus Gate

Damascus Gate is the most elaborate of the eight gates into the Old City. This creation of Suleiman rests upon the remains of a gate dated to the second century C.E. Situated on the north side of the Old City and the principal means of access to the Muslim and Christian sectors, the name of the gate in itself is a testimony to the diversity of those who use it and the controversy among them. Arabs call it "Bab el Amud" (Pillar Gate) for a pillar associated with the gate from which the distance to Damascus, the destination of the original road, was measured. Jews, particularly in recent years, call the gate "Shaar Shekhem" (Shechem Gate) because the road leads north to the site of biblical Shechem (now surrounded by the modern Arab city Nablus).

An hour at Damascus Gate provides enormous insight into Israel's diversity. It is difficult to describe the various sounds and smells on a busy morning. At the top and slightly to the west of the sloping entrance to the gate stands one of the largest taxi stands in Jerusalem. Horns honk; voices rise and fall as they haggle over fares. People—all manner of people— come and go. Around the entrance to the gate, vendors sell their wares. Much of it is common tourist stuff, but many different types of food add to the aroma of the place. There are animals—donkeys and, especially, cats; camels are seen less frequently in recent years. A delivery boy runs pell-mell down the sloping incline to the gate, his cart bouncing every few feet on a step while the load sways from side to side. Men, women, and children stream in and out of the gate, offering a panorama of the mainly Arab portion of Jerusalem.

Approximately 750,000 Arabs, or 18 percent of Israel's population of four and a half million residents, are citizens of Israel. Approximately another million Arabs live under Israeli control but are not citizens. Most of Israel's Arabs are Sunni Muslims, the larger of the two major sects of Islam and by far the largest group within Israel and Palestine. Arabs of the other group are known as Shiites and live mainly in Iraq and Iran. The division occurred shortly after the death of the Prophet Muhammad and originally centered on whether rulers (caliphs) could be descendants only of Ali, Muhammad's son-in-law (the Shiite position), or could be elected from Muhammad's tribe (the Sunni position). Today the Shiites consider themselves to be the more conservative and enthusiastic proponents of Islam.

The Arab population contains another major group—the Christians. They are Armenian Orthodox, Greek Orthodox, and Syrian Orthodox; Greek Catholics and Roman Catholics; Anglicans and members of several Protestant denominations (Baptists, Lutherans, Methodists, Presbyterians, and others). While not all the Christians in Israel are Arabs, a significant number of them are. Some Arab Christians trace their ancestry to pre-Islamic days in Palestine. Nazareth, for instance, the place of Jesus' childhood, is a largely Christian town of nearly forty thousand in the Galilee. Its Christian population has its roots in the early centuries of the Common Era. Christian Arabs occupy key positions in several municipalities, and they are particularly prominent in education and service agencies.

In general, the people streaming through the Damascus Gate are not prosperous. Their clothes are not stylish and are patched and well worn. Shopping bags contain mainly necessities. Eyes show a weariness and a wariness common to people for whom life is an unrelenting struggle. Some older Arab men wear full-length robes as outer garments as well as the traditional head dress, a *keffiyeh*. Most men, however, wear western-style suits, with and without a *keffiyeh*. While younger women and girls wear skirts and blouses, most of the older women wear long, loose-fitting, cloaklike gowns. Few Arab women in Israel wear veils. Among the throng one may see a Greek Orthodox priest in a long robe or Roman Catholic nuns in traditional garments. Those walking in and out include business and professional people going about their duties, shoppers, and school children.

## Arab Voices and Views

Were we to stop some of those hurrying by and ask why they are in this place and in this land, we would get a variety of responses. But to press them to *explain* why they are here can be interesting. The answers reflect values that are sometimes not so obvious.

Muyad, a fictional person drawn from interviews with many Arabs in Jerusalem, lives in a refugee camp near Bethlehem. A Muslim, he was not even born when the family fled from Jaffa (Joppa in the Bible) during the 1948 war. He and his family have lived in the camp for more than twenty years, which deeply colors his perspective. Now thirty-three, he works as a day laborer whenever he can get work. He longs to return to Jaffa. His grandparents and parents have described the family home, the neighborhood, the schools, the market. Never mind that the whole area has changed and that Jaffa is now a part of Tel Aviv. Never mind that many of the old homes have been torn down and that new streets, plazas, shops, and apartments have been built. To Muyad, it still exists and one day he hopes, expects, intends to return and claim what is his. He is at the Damascus Gate only because he cannot go home, home to Jaffa. But one day, he believes, he will. His birthright is a small parcel of land overlooking the Mediterranean Sea, and he intends to claim it. What's more, he will not be content until the whole of Palestine—the entire mandate ruled by Great Britain before 1948—is once again in Arab hands.

Miriam, a middle-aged Christian Arab, offers a similar account. Her village was destroyed decades ago. She is a teacher and has found her way to Jerusalem, where she lives with relatives. She has a deep commitment to assist her Palestinian neighbors, both Muslim and Christian. Unlike some of her friends who want to leave Palestine and go to the United States, Miriam feels a sense of vocation to Palestinian children. This place, this land, is theirs by right of occupation and biblical mandate. She vehemently denies Jewish claims to the land. She considers herself one of the rightful offspring of Abraham and Sarah. Her people were in Palestine long before it became modern Israel, and thus her sense of vocation is undergirded by a deep sense of belonging to this place. She has no dream of reclaiming and rebuilding her village in the Galilee, but she cannot imagine leaving her homeland. Her attitude toward Israel is resigned hostility.

For Paul, a seventy-year-old Armenian who has lived in Jerusalem his entire life, his passion for this place centers on the holy sites. He has watched as over the years more and more Christians have left. Political and economic hardships have driven many out, and the pressures have increased dramatically over the past decade. Paul grieves that those in the West do not seem to care about maintaining a Christian presence in Jerusalem. His forebears came as early as the fifth century C.E., but now the Christian population of Jerusalem and Israel as a whole is falling rapidly. Who will care for the ancient shrines? Who will maintain the ancient rites? If Christ is forgotten here, of all places, what hope can there be?

Faida, a young Arab woman of twenty, is from a small village south of Nablus. Her whole life has been lived under the Israeli occupation that began with the 1967 war. She and her family are Muslims and have struggled under the military administration. One of her brothers, arrested in a general roundup of Arab youths several months ago, is being detained by the authorities without specific charges. Faida has attended the university in Ramallah, which was closed by military order. She would not ordinarily be in Jerusalem but came in to visit relatives. She is intensely aware of the limitations that the occupation has placed on her generation. She wants Israeli forces to withdraw and allow her people to govern themselves. She dreams not about a return of land lost, but a release of land held captive. Faida's family was not driven out nor have they fled, but they live under military occupation and long for independence. They have land but are not free. Faida's dream is for her own nation, a Palestinian state, alongside Israel if need be, where Palestinians can have their own way of life, their own institutions, their independence. Israel has a right to exist, but it should allow Palestinians that same right and leave the occupied territories.

We could hear other Arab voices if we stayed long enough at Damascus Gate. An Israeli Arab would reflect on the difficulties posed by the dual identity of being Arab and a citizen of Israel. The 750,000 Israeli Arabs often feel they are second-class citizens in terms of educational and career opportunities. They do not serve in Israel's armed forces. Nonetheless, they are protected under Israeli law, have a passport, vote in Israel's elections, and can be elected to public office. Yes, we could hear other voices, but we must go to another gate, to Jaffa Gate, to listen to others, to Jews who make up approximately 80 percent of Israel's population.

## The People of Jaffa Gate

Jaffa Gate (*Shaar Yafo,* in Hebrew) is located in the western part of the Old City, and the road leading to Jaffa on the coast begins here. This gate is much less elaborate than Damascus Gate. A gap in the wall to the south allows small trucks to enter. While another gate, Dung Gate, gives easiest access to the Western Wall—the "Wailing Wall," the major Jewish religious site in the Old City—Jaffa Gate is an important entry point into the Jewish section of the Old City. It is not that Arabs cannot use this gate, which they call *Bab el Khalil* (Hebron Gate), nor that Jews cannot enter at the Damascus Gate; members of each group can and do use them. Local custom, however, keeps more Jews using Jaffa Gate and more Arabs at Damascus Gate.

The very existence of these two gates is a vivid symbol of the deep division between Jews and Arabs in Israel. Many Jews have little or no contact with Arabs. Even in Jerusalem, which has a large concentration of Arabs, it is possible to avoid serious contact almost completely. Arabs fill the menial-service and construction positions, but they can be ignored easily enough. This separation is underscored by the two gates. To be sure, Jaffa Gate is nearer the new part of Jerusalem where most Jews live, while Damascus Gate is opposite the older part of the city, mainly Arab East Jerusalem.

Jaffa Gate does not have the same hubbub as Damascus Gate; things at Jaffa Gate are more orderly. Sights, sounds, and smells caress the senses more than they assault them. The people going in and out are better dressed, and more family groups are seen walking together. The Jewish shops by and large sell a higher quality of merchandise. There are art galleries and archaeological excavations to visit, and nearby are several religious schools. All of these factors affect the number and kinds of people using Jaffa Gate. Time spent here offers insights that are as valuable as those gained at the Damascus Gate.

## Jewish Voices and Views

Rachel, for instance, is nineteen years old, a *sabra* (a native-born Israeli), in the second year of her mandatory military service. In her fatigues, with her weapon slung over her shoulder, she epitomizes a major segment of Israeli society. She has grown up in a world where constant military preparedness has been a necessity. She is determined that no one will destroy her nation, and the pride and confidence in her dark, flashing eyes are unmistakable. She would rather find a peaceful way to live with Arab neighbors and is ready for her government to negotiate appropriate borders. But when force is necessary, she believes it is fully justified. Like a majority of the Jews in Israel, she is not religious. For her, Jewishness is a matter of identity, not primarily a question of religious observance. She is Jewish, and her nation is Jewish. All Jews, secular and religious, have a place in Israel. Others are welcome so long as they acknowledge the right of Israel to exist as a Jewish state. Rachel believes she has a right to this land because she is here. She is Israeli! There is no other place to which she can or wants to go.

Bernie is the thirty-year-old son of parents who fled Nazi Germany in 1940. Many of his distant relatives died in the Holocaust. Life has not been easy for Bernie. His family was destitute when they arrived in Palestine. Eventually, after the 1948 War of Independence, Bernie's father opened a small grocery store. A few years after Bernie's birth, his father died. All his life, Bernie has struggled to get by. Now that his mother is dead and one of his brothers was killed during the Yom Kippur War in 1973, Bernie longs to go to the United States. He has a sense of loyalty to Israel and certainly hopes it will have a secure and fruitful future. But he wants out—out of military service, out of an economic situation marked by high inflation and limited opportunity, out of personal frustration. Bernie has no religious convictions that make it necessary for him to live in Israel. He can be as Jewish as he wants to be in the United States and would certainly have more opportunity to better himself financially. He keeps working and frankly hopes to meet an American woman who will marry him and provide him a way out of Israel. Bernie cares for his nation, but his personal situation is more compelling, and the United States looks like the answer.

David, forty-eight, is an American-born engineer who moved to Jerusalem fifteen years ago. He grew up on Long Island, went to school in Baltimore, and then worked there. He is a thoughtful, deeply religious man. After a trip to Israel to visit relatives and see the country, David decided to move here to participate in the miracle of Israel. Although he still retains his U.S. citizenship, he is certain that God is responsible for Israel's rebirth as a nation out of the horrors of the Holocaust and for the preservation of this small country despite the surrounding hostile powers. For David, Israel's right to exist is God-given; the deed to the land is in the Bible. He is enthusiastic about reinstituting nationally the biblical names, like Shechem for Nablus, Samaria and Judea for the West Bank. The appropriate boundaries are those of the kingdom of David and Solomon. Israel is God's special nation, and David is certain it will prevail.

Holding somewhat similar views but coming from quite a different background is Dvorah, fifty-three. She lives in a settlement about fifteen miles north of Jerusalem and comes to the city only rarely. Like David, she believes the land was God-given to Israel and thus is to be claimed to the exclusion of any who resist. Her reasoning, however, is somewhat different; she traces her ancestry through Jews who have lived in Palestine since before the Romans. Her ancestors were driven from Jerusalem by the Romans, but they did not leave Palestine. They moved to the Galilee, where they lived for centuries. During the late nineteenth century, Dvorah's grandparents returned to the outskirts of Jerusalem, where Dvorah was born. The War of Independence forced them to move to Tel Aviv for safety. To Dvorah, the land has always been occupied by Jews as testimony to God's promises. She is quick to share her family's history because, in her opinion, it establishes a prior claim to the land superior to that of any "latecomers" among the Arab population. She believes that Jewish rights to the land are better established than those of the Palestinians by reason of (1) the Bible and (2) continuous Jewish presence in the land. Her current goal is to settle and make Jewish all the territory that Israel has occupied since 1967. Arabs may or may not be welcome to live within Israel, depending on how they choose to relate to Israelis, but Israel's right to all the land west of the Jordan River is unquestioned in Dvorah's mind.

Moshe is an orthodox Jew. His long black coat, fur-lined hat, and *pieyot* (side-locks) indicate the Eastern European origins of his particular group. He belongs to a very strict orthodox sect whose members live in a part of Jerusalem called Mea Shearim. Moshe prefers to speak Yiddish, a language derived from High German. He believes Hebrew should be used only in prayer and in reading the Bible. A desire to be near the Wailing Wall and other holy places drew Moshe to Jerusalem some twenty years ago. Now, at the age of sixty-two, he is convinced that the state of Israel is the result of human rebellion, the work of human hands. Because only the Messiah can rightly restore Israel and bring back the Jews dispersed around the world, Moshe and his group refuse to acknowledge the legitimacy of the state of Israel. In his own eyes, he lives here in Jerusalem as a Jew, not an Israeli. His hope for a homeland can be fulfilled only with the Messiah's coming. In the meantime, Moshe is more concerned with the desecration of the Sabbath by secular Jews than with the threats of hostile Arab governments. In recent years, Ashkenazic Jews like Moshe (those whose roots are in Eastern Europe and Russia; most American Jews are of European origin and therefore Ashkenazic) have ceased to be the majority Jewish segment of Israeli society.

During the past thirty years, Sephardic Jews (those whose roots are in Spain, North Africa, and countries in the Middle East such as Iraq or Iran) have immigrated to Israel in large numbers and now constitute a majority of the Jewish population. These Sephardic Jews share much with Arabs in terms of culture because most grew up in Arab countries. Their Arab-like appearance and customs evoke suspicions among the Ashkenazim, who have been in the positions of power for most of modern Israel's national existence. The Sephardim as a group are less educated and less skilled. They have experienced a certain degree of discrimination as they have taken their place in Israeli society. In addition, they are largely secular Jews or are only minimally religious.

Yaacob is a Sephardic Jew born in Morocco. He came to Israel in 1965, in his late teens, and served in the military during the 1967 war. He is as fluent in Arabic as in Hebrew. Now in his early forties, he works as a tour-bus driver, a relatively good job in a sector of the economy that has suffered tremendously during the last several years. Yaacob is conservative in his political outlook. He does not question Israel's right to be in Palestine and will fight to protect his country. He is not hostile to Arabs in general—he grew up with Arabs and appreciates much in their culture—but he is convinced that Israel must deal from a position of power with any Arab governments that threaten Israel. While Yaacob is not a religious man, he is grateful for the state of Israel and sees it as a place where Jews can live in freedom as Jews. He accepts without much reflection the idea that the Jews of today are the continuation of the Israelites of the Bible. Thus it is appropriate for them to be here in Jerusalem and elsewhere in this land. Before uprisings in the occupied territories, Yaacob could conceive of an Israel where Jew and Arab could live together peacefully. Now he is not so certain.

Sasha has been in Israel for only a year. She is among the first of the new wave of Russian emigrants. She and her family could take very little with them when they left to come to Israel. Now she, her husband, who is a doctor, and their four children occupy a small two-bedroom apartment in one of the new communities encircling Jerusalem. She is grateful to be in Israel and is learning Hebrew. Like the Jews who came some years earlier from Ethiopia, Sasha's family cannot be said to practice traditional Judaism. She would be considered secular by religious Jews, but that in no way marks her attitude toward life. It merely testifies to her having spent most of her life in a country where she was not permitted to practice her religion. Her attitudes toward her new home are still being formed. Will she be more liberal because she now is living in a democratic society? Or will her attitudes be shaped by the reality that she never before had a voice— even a small voice—in the government? Will she support immigrants moving into parts of the land that are occupied primarily by Arabs, even if this means disregarding Arab claims of ownership? How will she relate to Arabs in general?

The impact of the number of Russian Jews moving into Israel cannot be assessed yet, but it will be significant. The government has estimated that by the end of 1993 more than a million new citizens will have joined the population. The changes that these new residents will cause are still unclear, but the effects on housing, health care, education, labor policies, and the political process will be great. The Sephardim will once again be in the minority with the Ashkenazim becoming a majority of almost three-quarters of a million.

## Still Other Peoples and Other Voices

Other groups live within Israel, but they are rarely seen at the gates of the Old City in Jerusalem. The Druse, whose first language is Arabic, live mostly in the northern districts of Israel and in the Golan Heights. In much larger numbers they are found in parts of Syria and Lebanon. The Druse have developed a religion that seems to combine elements of both Christianity and Islam, though details are shared only with the initiated. They tend to stay close to their home areas and are known as fierce fighters when it comes to protecting their own. Unlike Arabs (Israeli and non-Israeli), the Druse serve in the Israeli army and border police. The government of Israel has allowed the Druse a fair amount of autonomy. In return, the Druse have generally been good citizens of Israel. It is only in the Golan Heights, which belonged to Syria prior to 1967, where any problems seem to exist. The Druse who live in this area have strong cultural ties with the large number of Druse who live in Syria. These cultural ties are much stronger than the political divisions that geographically separate the Syrian Druse from the Israeli Druse in the Golan Heights. Loyalties are tested whenever Israeli or Syrian ambitions force the Druse to decide for Israel or Syria at the expense of other Druse.

The Bedouin, another group, primarily inhabit the Negev in the south of Israel. They are Arabs, and most are Muslims.

13

Their traditional lifestyle is radically different from that of most Israelis, Arab or Jew. The Bedouin culture is patriarchally organized in tribes. Women are veiled, marriages are arranged, and girls do not attend school. Until recently, the tribes roamed the desert freely with fierce independence and ignored most nationalistic pronouncements. They came into conflict with others, Arabs and Jews, only when their own tribal interests were threatened by nationalistic interests. Since 1967, however, Israeli policy has discouraged nomadic lifestyles. The Bedouin have found their movements restricted by the creation of new military bases, nature reserves, and settlements. Many of the younger people have never really known desert life, but work as day laborers in hotels, at construction sites, and the like. They resent their lost way of life and feel they are being treated unjustly by the government. They long not for a nation of their own, but rather for the freedom to move freely with their flocks and to preserve their lifestyle.

## Vital Diversity as the Norm

From this montage of individuals and their views, what can we learn about Israel, land, human rights, human hopes? Is there a single message or many messages? Given the wide variety of individuals and ethnic groups within Israel, clearly a number of important positions deserve recognition.

Both Jews and Arabs know a love for land; many have a genuine attachment to the land. Their identities are tied up with the land on which they live or to which they desire to return. For most, however, this is not a matter of philosophy or theology, but a much more concrete reaction to the realities of life. They want land on which to live and work. Those that have a place are committed to keeping it. Those who are without are determined to remedy that situation.

This issue has another level. Many Arabs and Jews possess nationalistic hope and pride. Many Jews, even those who do not want to live in Israel, are deeply proud of Israel as a nation. It is the homeland for Jews, a place where Jews can be Jews in safety and with dignity. The nation was established by international law, won and defended by military victory, and developed through hard work. Some Israelis trace their lineage to Jews who lived in the land in Roman times and even earlier. Israelis who may not agree on anything else are unified in their determination to protect their homeland.

Arabs also possess nationalistic fervor but obviously of a different sort. Some want to return to a bygone time when Israel did not exist. This wish is quite unrealistic. Others hope for some measure of autonomy, expressed preferably by a new nation for Arabs fashioned out of the occupied territories and coexisting with Israel. This is the hope that is at the base of the 1993 peace negotiations. Still others want only to be treated fairly and allowed to maintain their own culture with some independence. Basic to all of these notions is the fact that some Arab families, Muslim and Christian, have lived in Palestine for generations. Their sense of entitlement to the land is based on their tenure on it, sometimes legal title to it, and the conviction that the United Nations had no right to partition Palestine in the first place.

Most striking, though, is that relatively few have a well-developed religious notion or theology about land. When asked about their relationship to and understanding of Israel, most Arabs and most Jews answer at a secular level and emphasize nationalism or personal goals and desires. For non-Israeli Christians, this usually comes as a surprise, because many Western Christians talk about the Holy Land, the Promised Land, the land once given to ancient Israel and now restored by God to Jewish descendants of the first Israel. While some Israeli Jews express these sentiments, it is not nearly as frequent or important as Western Christians generally expect. Some use the religious and historical tradition to defend the establishment of a Jewish state in this particular place in the Middle East as opposed to some other part of the world, but the creation of the nation by the United Nations and the successful defense and development of the land are far more important to most Israelis than the religious claim.

Arab Muslims and Arab Christians usually reject any religious claim by Jews to the land. According to these Christians and Muslims, even if the land once was given to ancient Israel, it was lost because of disobedience. The ancient promise has no continuing value and certainly does not justify displacing Arabs in favor of Jews. Some Israeli Jews agree and disavow any religious claim on the land.

The rich diversity of people and opinion we have surveyed offers a brief, fundamental understanding of contemporary Israel. No single view concerning land emerges as normative. Efforts to articulate a theological perspective about land must begin with an acknowledgment of Israel's pluralism. Many opinions are expressed and are worthy of consideration. Formulations based on religion have often been more hurtful than helpful. Nonetheless there is a religious, a theological, dimension to the talk about land that cannot be ignored. Next, the histories of the people in the land of Israel may provide additional insight.

*For Further Reading*

Burrell, David and Yehezkel Landau, eds. *Voices from Jerusalem*. Mahwah, N.J.: Paulist Press, 1991.

Cragg, Kenneth. *The Arab Christian: A History in the Middle East*. Louisville, Ky.: Westminster/John Knox Press, 1991.

Friedman, Maurice. *Encounter on the Narrow Ridge: A Life of Martin Buber*. New York: Paragon House, 1991.

Friedman, Thomas L. *From Beirut to Jerusalem*. New York: Farrar, Straus & Giroux, 1989.

Shipler, David K. *Arab and Jew: Wounded Spirits in a Promised Land*. New York: Penguin Books, 1987.

# 2 | The Realities of History: People, Power, and Palestine

The contemporary country of Israel is home to numerous people. From many other places, they were drawn to Israel by religious motivation, the search for freedom and security, the hope of better economic opportunity, and combinations of these motives as well as others. Many people trace their lineage in the land through many centuries; they live now in a country called Israel, but their ancestors knew it by other names. Native-born, immigrants, refugees, victims of war, zealous settlers, cautious survivors, Jews, Muslims, Christians, secularists—they are all part of Israel and they ensure both vitality and conflict.

How this wide and rich variety of people came to be in Israel is important. Theological reflection apart from historical reality can foster grave misunderstanding if not outright error. Christians have all too often painted beautiful theological pictures while ignoring the harsh realities of time and place. Authentic theology requires serious and clear-sighted historical understanding. General theological statements about land may be fashioned, but any application of these principles will always be quite particular, specific, and concrete, requiring historical understanding and judgment. In choosing to use contemporary Israel as a focus of a broader theological consideration, some historical review becomes necessary.

A historical survey is all the more important because so much misunderstanding—indeed even ignorance—exists among North American Christians and others. Without some basic understanding of events, fair judgment—to say nothing of sympathy and compassion—is impossible. While Israel is often in the headlines, few readers seem to have bothered to acquaint themselves with the history that puts the headlines in proper perspective. Both bad theology and bad politics flourish when history is neglected or ignored.

To be sure, the writing of history is always biased to some degree. Choices of what to include, which sources to use, and whom to believe must be made. Absolutely "objective" historical reporting does not exist. No one—Christian, Jew, or Muslim—can be utterly neutral, but a level of fairness and accuracy can still be maintained. Fact and opinion are both important, and the way in which they are intertwined determines the trustworthiness and usefulness of a historical review. In this volume, I will discuss the legitimacy of Israel's existence alongside the ambiguity and complexity of much of Israel's history. At the same time, I acknowledge Palestinian cries for justice as well-founded, and I note Arab culpability for many of the difficulties of the Palestinians. Not every account would read this way. You, the reader, must judge the fairness and adequacy of the material.

The realities of our world situation affect our theological judgments. Conclusions suited for one situation may not fit another. The challenge of faith is to put the abstract formulations of theology into practical use, to live out what is preached. Thus, some history of the peoples of Israel is in order.

The Impact of Rome

The Roman siege had lasted for months. Within Jerusalem, competing groups of Jews had often clashed in the struggle to lead the resistance. When the walls were finally breached in 70 C.E. and the enemy stormed into the city, the horrors of war reached a climax. As the Jewish historian Josephus recounts in his *Wars of the Jews* 6.5, written between 80 and 90 C.E.:

While the holy house was on fire, everything was plundered that came to hand, and ten thousand of those that were caught were slain; nor was there a commiseration of any age, or any reverence of gravity; but children, and old men, and profane persons, and priests, were all slain in the same manner; so that this war went round all sorts of men, and brought them to destruction, and as well those that made supplication for their lives, as those that defended themselves by fighting. The flame was also carried a long way, and made an echo, together with the groans of those that were slain; and because this hill was high, and the works at the temple were very great, one would have thought that the whole city had been on fire. Nor can one imagine anything either greater or more terrible than this noise; for there was at once a shout of the Roman legions, who were marching all together, and a sad clamour of the seditious, who were now surrounded with fire and sword.

Thus, military and civilian inhabitants were slaughtered. The carnage was frightful. Fortifications, governmental quarters, the Temple—all were destroyed! Only a portion of the western wall of Herod's Temple survived, which centuries later became revered as the Wailing Wall. The revolt was over, a new era began.

The Dispersion

So it was that the Roman army under Titus overpowered and subdued Jerusalem in 70 C.E. The revolt had begun four years earlier. Roman response was immediate and brutal. The countryside was subdued first, and then the legions turned to Jerusalem, the symbol of religious and political independence. The Romans, by decimating the population and destroying the capital, inaugurated what has come to be known as the dispersion, or "Diaspora," of the Jews throughout the Roman Empire and eventually beyond. Centuries earlier (587 B.C.E.) the Babylonians under Nebuchadnezzar had dealt with rebellion in a similar manner, leveling Jerusalem (and many of the neighboring towns and villages) and taking the leadership of the city and nation into exile. The Jews who had escaped the ravages of the Roman conqueror in 70 C.E. were forbidden to rebuild Jerusalem and left to take up life elsewhere in the Galilee, Syria, Egypt, and other places around the Mediterranean Sea.

Power—brutal physical power—often defined the political realities of Palestine. From antiquity, people in the Middle East have brutalized one another. Memories of oppression and subjugation are nourished and preserved for decades, for centuries. The Jews of the Diaspora always remembered that they were exiled from their homeland by an enemy that brutally crushed their political and religious independence. Centuries passed with Jews all around the world remembering and praying for a day when they might once again return to the land of their historical beginnings and to Jerusalem. The plea and promise repeated in every Passover seder—Next year in Jerusalem!—never lost its meaning.

## Palestine

The land itself was given a "political" name, Palestine. To the forebears of the Jews expelled from Jerusalem in 70 C.E., the area had been known as Judea, and earlier as the land of Israel, *eretz Yisrael*. Before the Israelites took the land, it was the "land of Canaan." But the Bible never refers to this much-disputed territory as Palestine.

"Palestine" is derived from the name of one of ancient Israel's early enemies, the Philistines, who settled on the southern coast of Canaan. Herodotus, an ancient Greek historian, was apparently the first to use the word Palestine, a Greek form of Philistia, the country of the Philistines, as a designation for the area. After the attempted revolt of Jewish nationalist Bar-Kochba against Rome in 135 C.E., Roman emperor Hadrian removed the name Province of Judea from official records and monuments and used the name Province of Syria Palestine or Palestine in its place. Thus, Palestine became the region's name largely to punish the Jews and to remind them that they no longer controlled or had a claim to this territory.

Later, three provinces had the name *Palaestina*. Two were primarily west of the Jordan River (*Palaestina prima* and *Palaestina secunda*), and one was south and east (*Palaestina tertia*). Most of the province of Palestine was in Cisjordan (west of the Jordan), but some was in Transjordan (east of the Jordan). In the modern era, following World War I, the British revived the term Palestine for the land west of the Jordan (Cisjordan), which was under their rule. In 1923 they also created an emirate under British control in Transjordan, east of the Jordan River, now known as Jordan.

Today's difficulties over the land are all the more complex because, as early as the second century of the Common Era, the term Palestine designated the whole area now divided into Israel, Jordan, Lebanon, and Syria. Different people, depending on time, place, and political commitment, can mean and have meant different things when using the term Palestine. It is enough for us to remember that it is a term forcibly imposed, at least in part, for political reasons as a denial of Judean–Jewish claims on the territory.

## The Byzantine Era

Since the Romans, many rulers have exercised political and military power over Palestine. Under Constantine the Great (324 C.E.), Christianity became the established religion of the newly revived and reunited Roman Empire, and the Byzantine period began. Palestine became the Holy Land. Numerous holy places were identified and became the destination for Christian pilgrims. Jews were allowed limited access to Jerusalem, but only on the anniversary of the destruction of the Temple. At times during the years of Byzantine rule, conflicts broke out between the Christian rulers and Jews and Samaritans seeking independence (484, 526–65 C.E.).

In 614 C.E., Persians conquered Palestine, and some 37,000 Christians were taken prisoner to Persia. For fourteen years, Persia allowed Jews to rule Jerusalem again. The Christians who remained were given the choice of renouncing their faith or being killed. Power and politics at the service of religion continued to be the norm.

## Arab Rule Begins

Muhammad, the founder of the Islamic religion, was born around 570 C.E. He is called the Prophet of Islam and there are three spellings of his name: Muhammad, Mohammed, and Mahomet. By 632 C.E. when Muhammad died, Islam had spread throughout most of the Arabian Peninsula. Subsequently, the Muslims conquered the whole area that included the modern countries of Egypt, Iraq, Israel, Jordan, Lebanon, and Syria and eventually extended their empire as far west as Spain and as far east as India. The capital of the empire was placed in Damascus, Syria in 661 C.E. Arab rule of Jerusalem and Palestine was part of the conquest that began shortly after Muhammad died, and was firmly established in Jerusalem by 638 C.E.

Shortly after 1000 C.E., radical Muslim leaders began to persecute non-Muslims in Palestine, particularly Christians. The Church of the Holy Sepulchre in Jerusalem was destroyed in 1009, and the brutality encountered during the next several decades by Christians within Palestine and by pilgrims seeking to visit the Holy Land was one justification for the Crusades.

## The Crusades

Between 1099 and 1291, at least seven Crusades were launched to deliver the Holy Land from the hands of infidels, namely the Muslims. Atrocity was not limited to one side in these fierce conflicts, but Christians especially showed little understanding or discrimination in their attacks. Jews and

Muslims, civilians and combatants, often were slaughtered by the crusaders in the name of God and for the purpose of reclaiming control over the holy places sacred to Christian tradition. Eventually the Christian crusaders were repelled and Muslim rule resumed.

During the next two and a half centuries, Palestine was controlled by the Mamelukes, Muslims who came to power in Egypt around 1250 and extended their authority into Palestine after the crusaders were ejected. Under them, considerable building occurred. In 1492, Jews and Muslims were expelled from Spain, and many went east to Palestine.

The Ottoman Empire

Jerusalem was captured by Sultan Selim I, a Turkish Muslim leader, in 1517. Palestine became part of the Ottoman Empire, which extended across North Africa, to the south to Yemen, and through Greece to Hungary. Under Selim's son, Suleiman the Magnificent, new walls were built around Jerusalem, and those walls still surround the Old City. Turkish law became well-established and still is a factor in some disputes between Israelis and Palestinians. Ottoman rule extended for two centuries, but many of those years were marked by exploitation of natural resources, political mismanagement, and corruption. Toward the end of the Ottoman period, various European nations considered themselves patrons of different communities (especially Christians) living in Palestine.

In World War I, the Ottoman Empire was allied with Germany and lost Palestine in 1917 and 1918 to the British, who established a military administration. The League of Nations placed Palestine (territory that now is Israel and Jordan) under British mandate in 1920, and Syria (including modern Lebanon) under French mandate. The British mandate lasted through World War II and expired on May 15, 1948. This was a tumultuous period and directly influenced the events of the most recent forty years.

## Modern Zionism

Our historical survey must pause to consider one of the most significant movements to affect the history of the Middle East. In 1882, the first great wave of Jewish immigration to Palestine began, largely in reaction to oppression in Russia and Poland. This first "aliyah"—literally "going up" but meaning arrival in the area now known as Israel—was spurred by a group called Hoveve-Zion (lovers of Zion). This was the beginning of "practical Zionism," which aimed at establishing Jewish settlements in Palestine.

Shortly thereafter, Theodor Herzl, an Austrian Jew who was both journalist and playwright, launched "political Zionism" with the publication of his book *Jewish State* in 1896. Herzl's call for the creation of a Jewish national home in Palestine was prompted by the desperation he and other Jews felt as anti-Jewish feeling and discriminatory laws quickened across Europe.

Herzl's thinking was galvanized by the conviction of French army officer Alfred Dreyfus on trumped-up treason charges in 1894. Dreyfus, a Jew, was a victim of the anti-Jewish sentiment rampant in the army and elsewhere in French society. Although Dreyfus was fully exonerated after years of imprisonment, the affair was most sobering to Herzl. France might have been more progressive than other European nations, Herzl reasoned, but if Dreyfus could be so ill-treated, Jews had no place in Europe to enjoy full, first-class citizenship.

Therefore, Herzl dreamed of gathering Jews from around the world, and especially from Europe, to create a Jewish nation. His motive was political, not religious. The remedy for anti-Jewish repression was to create an independent Jewish nation where Jews could live safely while enjoying and perpetuating their culture. Herzl began his movement of political Zionism with the goal of attaining political recognition of a Jewish homeland.

In 1897, the First Zionist Congress was held in Basel, Switzerland, and a worldwide movement was organized to attract support for the right to a Jewish state. The goal was "to create for the Jewish people a home in Palestine secured by public law." Herzl died in 1904 and thus saw little fruit of his labors, but a movement had begun.

During the last years of the nineteenth century, a revival of Hebrew as a spoken and literary language began, and Zionism further encouraged this revival. Poetry, essays, and novels appeared, and a dictionary was produced. As Zionism proceeded, Hebrew became its language.

Practical Zionism remained primary until after World War I. From 1904 to 1914 a second major wave of Jewish immigration from Europe, the second aliyah, was organized. By 1914 nearly one hundred thousand Jews had settled in Palestine, alongside approximately six hundred thousand Arabs. In 1909 Tel Aviv was established as a purely Jewish city. Around 1910 the first kibbutz was organized. A vital Jewish presence was thus firmly rooted in Palestine.

Political Zionism took on new significance during World War I. After conquering Palestine, Great Britain pledged support for a Jewish national homeland in the Balfour Declaration of 1917. The statement was issued by British Foreign Secretary Arthur James Balfour as a part of an effort to gain Jewish support for Britain's campaign to control the Suez Canal. The declaration read:

> His Majesty's Government view with favour the establishment in Palestine of a national home for the Jewish people, and will use their best endeavors to facilitate the achievement of this object, it being clearly understood that nothing shall be done which may prejudice the civil and religious rights of existing non-Jewish communities in Palestine, or the rights and political status enjoyed by Jews in any other country.

This statement was endorsed by the League of Nations in 1922. Britain's mandate over Palestine was reaffirmed, but in 1923 the territory that now is Jordan was removed from the mandate.

The Balfour Declaration gave great impetus to political Zionism's goal of creating a Jewish homeland in Palestine. An organization called the Jewish Agency was recognized by Britain as the representative of Jews in Palestine. Cultural, educational, and economic institutions were created, and immigration was encouraged. Ever-increasing numbers of Jews came to Palestine, particularly after 1933 as the shadow of an anti-Jewish Third Reich grew longer. The exact numbers are much debated and are difficult to determine because of the way the records were kept, but the number of Jews grew dramatically.

Zionists interpreted the Balfour Declaration and the subsequent League of Nations mandate as a clear indication of Britain's intention and obligation to assist in the creation of an independent Jewish state. But others—including, as time went on, the British—did not. The British originally planned to create self-governing institutions for each of the various peoples settled in Palestine, including the large Arab majority. Arab leaders interpreted the declaration to mean that a Jewish state in Palestine could be established only if Arabs agreed to it. During the 1920s and 1930s, a number of Arab riots directed against Jews occurred as an expression of Arab opposition to establishing a Jewish homeland in Palestine.

Open rebellion by the Arabs against British rule began in 1936. For the next several years, efforts at compromise were made. Britain recommended in the Peel Report that Palestine be partitioned between Arabs and Jews, but this plan was rejected by the Arabs. In an effort to end the rebellion and to gain much-needed Arab support as the international situation deteriorated toward war, Britain decided in 1939 to limit the creation of Jewish settlements and to end all Jewish immigration to Palestine for five years. This action eventually proved Britain's undoing in the region. At the very moment when Jews most needed a safe place to which to flee from a well-orchestrated and well-organized campaign of genocide, the British closed the door to Palestine. Zionists and many other Jews were outraged. For the Arabs, it was too little too late. Britain's mandate did not end until 1948, but the troubles seen in the 1920s and 1930s would only increase.

It is important to note that not all Arabs were against all Jews. In numerous cases, Jews and Arabs lived peaceably side-by-side in cooperation and mutual respect, with each knowing the other's language. The politics of national states did not control these relationships.

Moreover, then as now, not all Jews were Zionists. Many Jews living in Palestine, as well as in Europe and the United States, rejected political Zionism on the grounds that only God could restore Jews to their homeland and would do so in God's time—not on some human time schedule. Many also insisted that Jews were a religious community and not a nationality. They did not view the establishment of a Jewish state as a religious obligation at all. They were not necessarily against the aims of Zionism, but they saw no reason to endorse them, either. A Jewish homeland in Palestine was not a first priority.

## The Division of Palestine

During World War II (1939–45), Arab and Jewish resistance to British rule was at a minimum. A greater threat was recognized, and many Palestinian Arabs and Jews joined the Allies in the struggle against the Axis powers. (A notorious exception was Mohammed Said Haj Amin el Husseini, who as mufti of Jerusalem was spiritual leader of Jerusalem's Muslim community and actively supported Adolf Hitler.) With the war's end, attention again centered on Palestine. Britain continued to limit Jewish immigration severely. The situation for Jews in Europe remained terrible. After the horror of the Holocaust, displaced Jews needed a place to go immediately. Desperate times fostered desperate action: Jews organized resistance—terrorism, opponents would say—against British authorities and installations. One of the most dramatic acts was the demolition of a wing of the famous King David Hotel in Jerusalem, which was being used as administrative headquarters by British military forces.

Britain took the matter to the United Nations in 1947, and the U.N. Special Commission on Palestine was established. This commission recommended that Palestine be divided into an Arab state and a Jewish state, with Jerusalem under international control and open to all. The proposed boundaries are shown on the map titled "U.N. Partition Plan." After much debate, the United Nations adopted this plan on November 29, 1947. The Jews quickly accepted the proposal, but the Arabs refused, arguing that the United Nations had no right to give away land that belonged to them. Hostilities broke out within Palestine but, more significantly, the Arab nations surrounding the disputed area vowed a war to drive the Jews out of the land and began preparations for it.

The British mandate was scheduled to expire May 15, 1948. On May 14, Palestinian Jews, led by David Ben-Gurion, proclaimed an independent state of Israel. The next day, as the British completed their withdrawal, troops from Egypt, Iraq, Lebanon, Syria, and Jordan (known as Transjordan until 1949) moved to support Palestinian Arab efforts to extinguish the newly proclaimed Jewish state. The Arabs had a tremendous military advantage over the much smaller, poorly equipped Jewish forces, but they lacked a unified command. Some Arab units were never deployed, and early opportunities to overrun Jewish positions were squandered. When the fighting ended months later, the Jews somehow had prevailed. The modern state of Israel had survived its first critical challenge.

In the course of the conflict some seven hundred thousand Arabs were displaced. Many fled their homes out of fear of atrocity—rumored or real—at the hands of some Jewish fighters. Others anticipated a quick Arab victory and expected to return when the fighting was over. Instead, these refugees were to begin a long sojourn in neighboring Arab countries. For many of their children and grandchildren, the exile continues. At the conclusion of the fighting, Israel controlled—in addition to land designated for the Jewish state under the United Nations' plan—the western half of Jerusalem and about half of the land designated by the U.N. for Arab control. This is shown on the map titled "Israel after 1948–49 War." Egypt and Jordan controlled the rest of the territory known as Palestine under the partition plan. Those areas came to be called the West Bank (Jordanian territory west of the Jordan River) and the Gaza Strip (the area around Gaza on the Mediterranean coast, about forty-five miles south of Tel Aviv, which was controlled by Egypt).

On January 15, 1949, the United Nations negotiated a number of armistices to establish peace. The borders were drawn along the cease-fire line but were not recognized by the Arabs. Israel elected its first government, with Chaim Weizmann as president and David Ben-Gurion as prime minister. The first census taken by Israel in 1948 totaled approximately 872,000, including about 150,000 Arabs who had not fled at the outbreak of the fighting. Power and politics had once again rearranged the political geography of Palestine. A new nation, Israel, proclaimed as a homeland for Jews who had been scattered across the face of the globe for almost two millenia, took its place in world politics.

## Securing the Borders

The early years of modern Israel's existence were difficult. Large numbers of immigrants arrived and had to be settled; an economy had to be built. Without the assistance of the governments of the United States, Great Britain, and West Germany, in particular, and the contributions of Jewish communities and individuals from around the world, Israel could not have survived.

In addition to the stress of establishing the nation in an area with few natural resources and a limited work force, Israel was further confronted by hostile neighbors and no readily defensible borders. Armed attackers could easily penetrate Israel and did so frequently.

Matters came to a head in 1956. For several years, Egypt had been supporting attacks on Israel from the Gaza Strip,

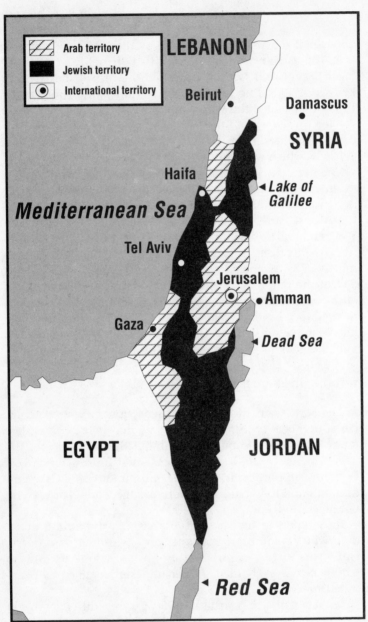

Map 1. U.N. Partition Plan

Map 2. Israel after 1948–49 War

and Israel responded in kind. Because Israeli shipping was not allowed to pass through the Suez Canal, Israel had developed Eilat as its seaport on the Gulf of Aqaba. Egyptian artillery easily controlled the entrance to the gulf, however, and posed a threat to ships bound to or from Israel. In July 1956, Egypt seized the Suez Canal from the British and French who then controlled it, thus tightening the screws on Israel's economy.

On October 29, 1956, Israel invaded Egypt. The English and French, as prearranged, joined the fray in a very limited way and reclaimed the Suez Canal. Israel's army and air force soon overcame all other Egyptian resistance. By November 5, Israel's forces occupied the Gaza Strip and the Sinai Peninsula and had opened the Suez Canal and Gulf of Aqaba to Israeli shipping. The United Nations arranged cease–fires and assigned U.N. troops to maintain them. Israel withdrew its forces but had demonstrated its ability to defend its borders with military power.

Eleven years later, border violations once again precipitated a full-blown conflict. The United Nations had been able to reduce drastically the incursions along the Egyptian–Israeli border, but attacks and counterattacks along the borders between Israel and Syria and Israel and Jordan became steadily more frequent and destructive. The rhetoric of war, punctuated by armed clashes, reached a peak in 1967. Arab newspapers and radio stations clamored for a war of annihilation against Israel. Israel, and many of its supporters in the United States, feared for the nation's survival.

In May 1967, Egypt's President Gamal Abdel Nasser declared a blockade of Israeli shipping and prohibited strategic materials on non-Israeli vessels from the Straits of Tiran, which control access to Eilat. Israel tried diplomatic means to lift the blockade, but to no avail, and on June 5, 1967, Israeli planes launched a surprise attack on several critical airfields in Syria, Jordan, and Egypt. Within hours, Israel almost completely destroyed the Arab nations' air power. Fighting in this brief conflict, known as the Six-Day War, was fierce. By June

10, Israeli troops had occupied the Gaza Strip, the Sinai Peninsula up to the Suez Canal, Jordanian territory west of the Jordan River, and Syria's Golan Heights. Israel immediately proclaimed East Jerusalem, controlled by Jordan since the 1948 conflict, to be a part of Israel.

At the cease–fire, Israel held territory equal to three times its size before the war, as shown in the map titled "Israel and the Occupied Territories after the 1967 War." Thousands of people fled from East Jerusalem and the West Bank. The Palestine Liberation Organization, then the leading political voice of the Arab population, became all the more determined to regain homesteads abandoned in the flight before the advancing Israelis. The Arab refugee population was greatly expanded and largely unassisted. The Arab countries to which they fled did not assimilate them, restricting them mainly to overcrowded, poorly equipped camps. United Nations Resolution 242, passed on November 22, 1967, called for a return to prewar boundaries and recognition by all parties of the rights of each other, including Israel, to exist in secure borders and at peace. More than a quarter century would pass before the first significant steps would be taken in 1993 toward fulfilling the latter part of the resolution.

By 1973 tension once again reached an intolerable level. Border fighting exploded into all-out war on October 6, when Egypt and Syria launched simultaneous attacks on Israel. The date was Yom Kippur, the Jewish Day of Atonement, and the most important of Jewish holidays. Fierce fighting and heavy casualties occurred in the Sinai Peninsula and the Golan Heights. In November 1973, Israel and Egypt agreed to a cease-fire, but the fighting between Syria and Israel continued until June 1974. Israel had penetrated both Egyptian and Syrian territory but agreed to withdraw to prewar borders. A buffer zone along the Suez Canal and in the Golan Heights, patrolled by U.N. forces, was established.

Israel had once again proved able to defend its borders, but at heavy cost. The Yom Kippur War, as this conflict was called, clearly demonstrated Israel's military prowess, but it also revealed much unrest in the nation. Israelis had not experienced the same level of casualties in either the 1956 Suez War or the 1967 Six-Day War as they had in the Yom Kippur War. The government's handling of events prior to and during the conflict was criticized. Golda Meir, who had been prime minister since 1969, resigned in 1974. The economy was under great pressure. Three years later, in 1977, the Labor Party, which had controlled the government since independence, was ousted in favor of the Likud Party.

The new government, under the leadership of Prime Minister Menachem Begin, immediately began to seek political resolution of disputes with its neighbors. Anwar el Sadat of Egypt responded. Eventually, through the mediation of U.S. President Jimmy Carter, Begin and Sadat signed the Camp David Accords. A peace treaty between Egypt and Israel was signed March 26, 1979, and Israel began a withdrawal from the Sinai Peninsula that was completed in 1982.

One important provision of the Camp David Accords was never accomplished. Self-government for the Gaza Strip and West Bank was to have been established for five years, after which a final decision was to be made on their status. Details could not be agreed upon, however. On July 30, 1980, Israel declared Jerusalem to be "capital of Israel for all time," an action still not recognized by the United States and many other governments around the world. In 1981, Israel announced the formal annexation of East Jerusalem and the Golan Heights, which it had occupied since 1967. The West Bank and Gaza continued under military rule.

## The Palestine Liberation Organization

At the end of Israel's 1948 War of Independence, approximately seven hundred thousand Arabs who had previously resided in territory claimed by the new state were living in Arab countries, principally Lebanon, Syria, Jordan, and Egypt. These refugees had one overriding goal: to return to their homes. Of course, this required that Israel be eliminated.

Map 3. Israel and the Occupied Territories after the 1967 War

Unrest and hate of Israel filled the camps where these thousands of displaced Arabs lived. The major Arab governments used these people as pawns in their designs against Israel.

In 1964, the Arab heads of state created the Palestine Liberation Organization (PLO) as a way of controlling the Palestinians living in their countries. The charter of the PLO, written in Cairo, refused to acknowledge Israel as a state. It stated that the land of Palestine was Arab land and the Jews had no right to any part of it. The charter pledged unending hostility against Israel until all Arab land was restored to its true owners. The Jews would be driven out so that Arabs could return.

As events unfolded during the 1950s and 1960s, the PLO's goals seemed less and less realistic. Israel was clearly able to defend itself. Prior to the 1967 Six-Day War, most Arab refugees were from areas within the borders that Israel had established in 1948. To return to these places was not possible without the destruction of Israel, and each war made that seem less likely.

Even before the PLO was created, groups had been formed for the purpose of liberating Palestine. One of the first was al-Fatah (Victory), created in Kuwait in 1956 by a group of middle-class Palestinians whose spokesman was Mohammed "Yasir" (a nickname meaning "easy" that was given him as a child) Arafat. Al-Fatah carried out numerous attacks on Israel during the 1960s. Although other groups existed, Arafat's organization was the most successful and best known.

Arafat's reputation grew, and in 1969 he was able to gain control of the PLO from the Arab governments. He turned it into an organization truly concerned with the Palestinian cause. In 1974 the Arab governments acknowledged the PLO as the "sole, legitimate representative of the Palestinian people;" the United Nations also recognized the PLO that year. Israel, not surprisingly, refused to recognize or deal with the PLO and maintained this stance until the secret negotiations, which began early in 1993, culminated with the mutual recognition of Israel and the PLO.

Under Arafat the PLO became an organization with considerable power. Arab governments contribute large amounts of money to it annually, and the PLO has a multibillion–dollar investment portfolio that generates more than $200 million a year for the PLO's operating budget. Radio stations, newspapers, educational programs, scholarships, health payments, diplomatic missions, weapon purchases—all are made possible through the PLO. Indeed, some sixty thousand Palestinian families are directly dependent upon the PLO for their well-being.

## The Invasion of Lebanon

During the 1970s, the PLO had its base of operations in Beirut, Lebanon. Jordan's King Hussein drove the PLO militia from Jordan in 1970 (because their raids against Israel led to Israeli retaliation against Jordan), and as a result, Syria and Lebanon saw a great influx of Palestinians. Tensions moderated between Jordan and Israel considerably, but not between Lebanon and Israel. Lebanon's civil war was beginning in 1975 and generated further difficulties for Israel because no authority was able to prevent attacks from across the Lebanese border. PLO military units situated in Lebanon acted with complete freedom to strike against Israel.

On June 6, 1982, Israel invaded Lebanon, with the goal of annihilating the PLO. Within a week, the Israeli army reached Beirut and besieged it. In the following months, Arafat reluctantly signed a declaration which included an acknowledgment of Israel's right to exist. In exchange, remnants of the PLO forces were evacuated from Beirut that August. The PLO had not been eradicated, but certainly the organization's power had been greatly curtailed.

The Israeli army eventually was withdrawn from Lebanon in 1985, but it maintained a partial presence, as indicated on the map titled "Israel's borders as of 1985." During the occupation, several events both memorable and horrible took place. In September 1982, with Israeli army units providing

37

cover, Lebanese Christian militiamen entered two Palestinian refugee camps, Sabra and Shatila, and mercilessly slaughtered hundreds of people. The victims were mostly women and children. When news of this horror reached Israel, four hundred thousand Israelis demonstrated in Tel Aviv on September 24 to demand the resignation of the government and prosecution of those directly responsible for the massacre.

The other event illustrates the chaotic and brutal situation in Beirut during Israel's occupation of Lebanon. United States Marines arrived in August 1982 to stabilize the situation and support the government then in power. The Marines' movements and authority were greatly restricted, and while they were initially received enthusiastically by the Lebanese, eventually they became identified with "one side." The climax came on October 23, 1983, when a truck carrying 12,000 pounds of dynamite was driven into the Marine headquarters, where it exploded, killing 241 U.S. soldiers who were acting as peacekeepers. In February 1984, the Marines were withdrawn.

Today, many Israelis regard the invasion of Lebanon as a costly mistake. The government that planned and carried it out was forced out of office, with Defense Minister Ariel Sharon resigning on February 2, 1983, and Prime Minister Begin on September 9, 1983. While Israel's goal of securing the border of Lebanon could be understood, the invasion went well beyond that. Initially a military victory, the invasion was a political disaster. The Israeli populace was angered and embarrassed. Moreover, support for Israel in the United States dropped significantly because of the massacres at Sabra and Shatila. And, after the Beirut bombing of the Marines, many Americans were ready to get out of the Middle East altogether.

The slaughter in the refugee camps had an unexpected effect on the people living under military rule in the West Bank and Gaza Strip. The PLO had left the civilians in the camps unprotected, and it had withdrawn from Lebanon. West Bank and Gaza Strip Palestinians came to realize that, with the humiliation of the PLO military, they could count on

Map 4. Israel's borders as of 1985

no one but themselves. An even more-dedicated Palestinian nationalism arose from Israel's invasion of Lebanon.

## The Uprising

Four days in December 1987 produced a profound change in the relation between Israel and the million-plus Arabs who lived in the West Bank and Gaza Strip. First, an Israeli shopper, Shlomo Sakle, was fatally stabbed by a Palestinian in Gaza on December 6. Next, a runaway Israeli truck killed four Palestinian workers from the Jabaliya refugee camp in Gaza and injured seven others on December 8. The following day, a disorder ended with Israeli soldiers killing a seventeen-year-old Palestinian boy, Hatem Abu Sisi. Like a match to tinder, these events touched off the uprising (in Arabic, the *intifada*). The protest that erupted in the Jabaliya camp quickly spread throughout the West Bank. On December 21, a solidarity strike was mounted by the seven hundred thousand Arabs who were Israeli citizens. The anger that had been smoldering and building during twenty years of military occupation was released. Things would not be the same again.

The *intifada* surprised everyone. The Israelis could not at first believe it was a genuine, internally led uprising and tried to blame it on outsiders. They tried to deny its wide support, but it continued unabated. The more the military tried to enforce cooperation, the less it achieved. Some have argued that the Israeli authorities showed restraint, and it is true that the best-equipped military in the Middle East could have inflicted far more damage had it been allowed or encouraged to do so. Amnesty International reported that in 1992 Palestinians killed more than 200 of their own people who were suspected as being collaborators, while Israeli forces killed only 120. Nonetheless, despite such statistics, the Arab population, particularly the young, suffered far too many deaths and injuries as an ever more frustrated Israeli military tried unsuccessfully to break the resistance.

The *intifada* also surprised the Arab world outside Palestine and particularly the PLO. No one expected the Palestinians in the Gaza Strip and the West Bank to take their future into their own hands. The PLO had no role in launching or leading the uprising. In November 1988, nearly a year after the *intifada* began, the Palestine National Council (the PLO's parliament in exile) acted to support the uprising by declaring an independent Palestinian state, though borders were not drawn.

The *intifada* probably surprised the Palestinians in the Gaza Strip and West Bank most of all. For twenty years they had talked a lot, but done little. Individuals had occasionally resisted, but not communities. Palestinians had talked of being a people, but had not mobilized. Then almost overnight, Palestinian consciousness and unity took a giant step forward. The resistance was actually quite controlled. Rocks can and did inflict fatal injuries, but they were no match for rifle fire. The economic shutdowns and the orchestrated rock-throwing incidents that marked the *intifada* as it moved through its second year were designed more to build a sense of unity within the Palestinian community than to inflict serious injury on Israel. By rising up as they did, the Palestinians living under Israeli military occupation said: "No more! We are a people!"

The situation was complicated by the policy of the Likud Party under the leadership of Yitzhak Shamir, which stepped up the creation of Jewish settlements within the occupied territories as a response to the *intifada*. The West Bank was now routinely called Samaria (a biblical name) by many Israelis, implying that this area was to be viewed as belonging to modern Israel, as it did to ancient Israel. These Jewish settlements in the midst of a largely hostile Palestinian population increased tension.

The final outcome of the *intifada* is yet to be seen, although any peace accord between the PLO and Israel certainly will have some effect. Many Israelis are sympathetic to the Palestinians. Many more, however, insist that the security of Israel

41

is most important and must be guaranteed. Many still believe that power will prevail if only applied with sufficient severity, and many Israelis, including the settlers, demonstrated against a prospective Israeli–PLO accord in September 1993. Among the Palestinians, their determination seems undiminished, and many expressed concern that the process of self-government will proceed too slowly.

Most observers hope for a political solution. Peace talks, which began in the fall of 1991 and included the Israeli government, Palestinians from the occupied territories, and several Arab governments, were further stimulated by the election of Yitzhak Rabin of the Labor Party as Prime Minister of Israel.

The Palestine Declaration of Independence implicitly recognized Israel's right to exist in peace and security, and Arafat did so explicitly on December 14, 1988, though the PLO Charter has yet to be altered to reflect such a change in policy. Thus, some forty years after a war intended to annihilate the Jewish state, this Arab group has in effect accepted the United Nations 1947 partition plan and the subsequent U.N. Resolutions 242 and 338, which call all parties to acknowledge the others' right to a secure state with peace. This was affirmed even more dramatically five years later when, on September 13, 1993, Arafat and Rabin shook hands after the signing of an accord of mutual recognition and an outline for advancing peace negotiations. In Norway, early in 1993, the deal had been developed in secret meetings lasting several months. It was culminated publicly in Washington, D.C. in the presence of President Bill Clinton and a group of well-wishers.

The events of 1993, while by no means conclusive, may foreshadow a new day. Certainly, conditions within Israel and within the occupied territories are unlike they have ever been. The *intifada* has resulted in a Palestinian people more united than ever before, and many Israelis clearly question the economic, human, and moral costs of continuing the conflict.

## A New Setting for Understanding

The election of the Labor Party and the *intifada* were not the only sources of pressure for peace. Russia, the largest and most powerful country to emerge from the collapse of the former Soviet Union, has encouraged the peace talks. And the demise of the Soviet superpower, which had supported some Arab nations militarily, may yet play a role in resolving the Middle East conflicts. American politics certainly contributed to hopes for peace in 1993. PLO officials said they moved toward an agreement with Israel because they believed President Bill Clinton's government was more pro-Israeli than any administration in the last quarter century. But the shape of the future remains unclear. Will there be two states? One? None?

Whatever the result, judgments will be made and actions will be initiated that are based, in part, on theological perspective. The theology may be implicit or explicit, uninformed or intentional, denied or openly articulated, but some measure of theological opinion will be at work. For Reformed Christians, the Bible provides another major source by which historical action is informed. While always fashioning judgment on the basis of history's realities, Reformed Christians also listen carefully to the Bible for its challenge to our prejudices and its declaration of God's values and agenda. Therefore, a review of biblical teaching concerning land is next.

### For Further Reading

Collins, Larry and Lapierre, Dominique. *O Jerusalem!* New York: Simon & Schuster, 1972.

Friedman, Thomas L. *From Beirut to Jerusalem.* New York: Farrar, Straus & Giroux, 1989.

Johnson, Paul. *A History of the Jews.* New York: Harper/Collins, 1988.

Rudin, A. James. *Israel for Christians.* Philadelphia: Fortress, 1983.

Yapp, M. E. *The Near East Since the First World War.* White Plains, N.Y.: Longman Publishing Group, 1990.

# 3 | God and Earth-keeping: Biblical Perspectives on Land

The Bible has much to say concerning land: from accounts about God's creation of all the land to disturbing examples of individuals and groups moving in and taking land by force from others; land promises, land gifts, land crimes, land losses. The result is that the Bible presents a picture of a God who is involved with people and land and justice and deliverance, a God who creates a good world and who intends all mortals to live in it responsibly and peaceably.

This chapter explores some of the many texts that address issues involving land to gain some perspective on what is at stake from the Bible's viewpoint when we speak of the Promised Land, the land of Israel, land rights, the Holy Land, and God's Land. Why indeed should we think about the Bible at all in connection with a modern, geopolitical entity, Israel?

## The Bible and Ethical Judgment

Let's begin with the last issue. Why should we consider the Bible when we struggle with such modern issues as territorial disputes between nations or between ethnic groups, as occurred in the former Soviet Union and the former Yugoslavia? How will the Bible help or hinder such a consideration? Is there a single, clear-cut answer to questions about water rights, military occupation, civil disorder, and the multitude of concerns with which real, live people in Israel must deal?

In shaping a response to these questions, it is important to recognize our limits. The Bible was not written with contemporary Israel as its focus. It was written thousands of years ago in a much different historical and social setting. In that respect, the Bible is dated, an antiquity that may be interesting but little else. The Bible is not a legally binding land grant nor a blueprint to a predetermined future waiting irresistibly to unfold.

On the other hand, however, the Bible is a book treasured, cherished, read, and reread by two significant faith communities in our modern world. For Jews, the Bible comprises the books that Protestants call the Old Testament. For Christians, the Bible obviously includes the New Testament as well. For Catholic and Orthodox Christians, the Bible also contains material in the Old Testament, called the Apocrypha, which neither Jews nor Protestants acknowledge as part of the Bible. (It should be noted that Muslims also honor the books of the Old and New Testament, though they claim that significant alterations should be made to properly understand these books.) Despite differences which clearly exist between Jews and Christians with respect to the whole collection of materials that is generally called the Bible, it is true that both faith communities hold the Bible in special regard and honor it as God's word.

For some, the "word" is equated with the "words." For others, God's word is heard as the community responds by interpreting and obeying the ancient word in contemporary settings. The Bible seldom if ever can be applied directly and literally to answer concrete, complex legal and ethical questions simply, but it does provide guidelines and direction; it suggests the right questions to ask as people of faith struggle to be faithful.

For people active in faith communities, the issue is not *whether* to consider the Bible when dealing with the tough questions of life, but *how*. The approach taken in this volume is to consider the Bible carefully with the intent of gaining understanding. The task is not to determine which view is correct, oldest, or most authoritative. Rather, the goal is to listen and reflect upon the events that God's people have experienced and passed along in the hope and with the conviction that God continues to care for and give guidance to those who seek to place God's agenda foremost in their lives.

It is important to note at the outset, however, that the theme of human responsibility before God is found throughout the biblical accounts. Much less is said about land rights than about the allegiance owed to God by all human beings, by those whom God has set as earth-keepers in the midst of creation. Responsible, just action within God's land and care for the land become the guiding norms. Such responsibility must be brought to reality in the real, historical world of politics and power, and thus the success or failure of every attempt at dominion can be measured against the Bible's call for righteousness, for love, for mercy, for justice, for the God-fearing exercise of the full range of responsibilities that God has given to human earth-keepers appointed for this purpose.

## The Promised Land

The promise of land is one of the basic themes found first in Genesis and echoed in other parts of the Bible. Abram and Sarai at God's command leave the country of their families on a quest for "the land that I will show you" (Gen. 12:1). With the promise of becoming a great nation, famous, and a blessing for many, the forebears of the people of Israel set out from southern Mesopotamia eventually to find their way to the land of Canaan, which would later be called Palestine (Gen. 12:4–6). When they reached "the land," God appeared to Abram and gave a promise that was to encourage and guide countless people for centuries to come: "To your offspring I will give this land" (Gen. 12:7).

The narrative concerning Abram and Sarai is well known and is built around the promise of posterity and land given by God. There are threats to Abram and Sarai (Gen. 12:17–20, 13:8–18, 14:13–16, 20:8–18). Covenants are made (Gen. 15:17–21, 17:1–14), new names, Abraham and Sarah

(Gen. 17:5, 15), are given, but the promises of land and posterity are repeated at each new step on the way (Gen. 12:7, 13:14–17, 15:5, 7, 18–21, 17:4–8). The drama reaches its climax when Isaac, the long-awaited though not really expected heir of Abraham and Sarah (15:2–4, 16:1–4, 17:16–21, 18:9–15, 21:1–7) is designated as the offering that God wants Abraham to make as a sign of his allegiance (Gen. 22:1–2). At the last moment, however, Abraham is stopped from carrying out the horrible deed and is once again given the divine assurance of posterity and land (Gen. 22:9–18).

In the all-too-human stories of the descendants of Abraham and Sarah, each new generation is again met by God and given promises of children and land: first Isaac (Gen. 26:3–4) and then Jacob (Gen. 28:3–4, 13–15, 35:9–12). The promise is remembered at the death of Jacob (Gen. 48:21), and again when Joseph's days are over (Gen. 50:24). Centuries later, when God encounters Moses at a burning bush, the divine self-identification includes a reference to those to whom the promise had been made generations earlier (Ex. 3:6, 15). The offspring of Abraham and Sarah, though enslaved in Egypt, were not forgotten. God sent Moses to lead them out and to guide them to the land promised first to Abraham and Sarah, the land of the Canaanites (Ex. 3:8, 15–17, 6:3–8). The theme of promised land continues until it is fulfilled in Joshua with Israel's entry into Canaan (Josh. 24:1–13).

The promise to Abraham and Sarah was remembered long after its fulfillment at the time of Joshua. It was included in the rendition of God's faithfulness in Psalm 105 and in Ezra's recital before the people after the return from exile (Neh. 9:7). God's faithfulness to the promise is noted at the time of Jesus' birth in Luke 1:55, 73. That the promise included blessing that would flow through Abraham to all peoples (Gen. 12:3, 22:18, 26:4, 28:14) was remembered as well (Isa. 19:24; Zech. 8:13; Acts 3:25; Gal. 3:8–9).

In the traditions of promised land, it's essential to recognize the this-world character of the divine commitment.

While the fulfillment of the promise that led Abram and Sarai out of Mesopotamia lay in the future, the land they were to seek was real land, territory in this world, not just a metaphorical place. Across the centuries, Jews interpreted the promise of a land in many ways, but for most the real, this-world Jerusalem, at least, continued to have special significance. Jerusalem was not only a symbol but a real place where people could live and work and worship. God's promise represented an intention that the people would have a place in this world where they could live out their lives fully as God's people.

For many Christians, either the promise of land was spiritualized—understood as a reference to a spiritual reality, such as heaven—or it was ignored altogether. For many Western Christians, the notion of a special, God-promised land was seen as an unworthy relic of a narrow, particularistic religion (meaning Judaism), which they believed had rightly been recognized as nonessential by the more enlightened universalism of Christianity. The Eastern Church, however, continued to celebrate the specialness of Jerusalem and Palestine, though in ways that all too often ignored or disdained Jewish understandings of the biblical tradition. Nevertheless, the material, this-worldly aspect of God's gifts was maintained and honored. The spiritual and the worldly met at particular times in real places, and that is of significance.

## The Land of Israel

From the beginning of recorded history, people have lived along the eastern coastline of the Mediterranean Sea. For several thousand years before Abraham and Sarah—who in turn lived at least five hundred years before the emergence of the people called Israel—people worked the land, raised flocks, developed various trades, fought with one another occasionally, and did all the other things that mark human societies. These were not modern people, to be sure, but they were not primitive, either. They left written records of their culture in some instances and numerous artifacts attesting to their presence in the land.

By the time the Bible was taking shape, these people had come to be called Canaanites (Gen. 10:19, 24:3; Deut. 1:7, 11:30; Neh. 9:24) or in a more specific manner the population was said to include "the Kenites, the Kenizzites, the Kadmonites, the Hittites, the Perizzites, the Rephaim, the Amorites, the Canaanites, the Girgashites, and the Jebusites" (Gen. 15:19–20). The land of Canaan was a common term of reference.

Into the land of Canaan, the territory occupied by men, women, and children referred to as Canaanites, came the people of Israel. The historical evidence is not conclusive about precisely when or how Israel moved in. The biblical narrative in some places suggests that Israel's occupation resulted from a decisive series of battles under the leadership of Joshua (Josh. 6, 8, 10—11). Other biblical verses, however, make clear that the process was not as unambiguous as it first appears (Josh. 13:1–7, 13, 16:10, 17:12; Judg. 1:27–33). Further, they had competition for the land from the Philistines, who moved in on the coast after failing in their attempt to enter Egypt. From the biblical witness and archaeological work, we know that one group of people, generally termed Canaanites, was displaced or brought under domination of another group, the Israelites, across a time span of approximately two hundred years. Sudden battles, gradual encroachment, treaties, intermarriage, trade—all of these seem to have played a part. But the end result is clear: the land of Canaan became the land of Israel.

The process culminated with the crowning of David, son of Jesse, as king (2 Sam. 5:1–5). For some two hundred years, the people had been loosely associated as clans that occasionally acted in concert, usually for defense (Judg. 5). Saul, a Benjaminite, was chosen as the first king of Israel (1 Sam. 8–12), but he had only moderate success in bringing the people together. Under David a unified government was instituted. David, first recognized as king by Judah (2 Sam. 2:1–4), created a government that utilized clan or tribal allegiance but went beyond it. Jerusalem, a Jebusite or Canaanite city belonging to none of the tribes, was captured and made the capital (2 Sam. 5:6–10). The Ark, the symbol of God's presence, was brought to Jerusalem as a sign of the new unity (2 Sam. 6). David consolidated his borders (2 Sam. 8–10) and thus began what we call the "united kingdom," which lasted approximately eighty years with the northern and southern tribes ruled effectively by one king—first David and then his son Solomon.

During the united monarchy, the kingdom reached its maximum size. The phrase "from Dan to Beersheba" expressed the extent of Israel's territory (Judg. 20:1; 1 Sam. 3:20; 2 Sam. 24:2, 6, 15) indicating the far north to the far south. David is remembered as extending his rule to the east of the Jordan River over Moab, Ammon, Edom, and part of Syria, while also bringing the Philistines on the coastal plain under his control (2 Sam. 8, 10). Solomon maintained David's conquests and pushed the border southward to the Gulf of Eilat (or Aqaba), which leads into the Red Sea. The Negev or southern desert became part of the kingdom. Thus, at its largest, Israel extended from Eilat in the south almost to Mt. Hermon in the north, and from the Mediterranean on the west to the Jordan River on the east. Further, Israel effectively exercised political control over some parts of the nations east of the Jordan.

The question of borders is important. Some modern Jews and Christians contend that modern Israel has a right to the territory claimed at the time of Solomon's kingdom. The biblical sources are difficult to interpret, however, and leave questions (Ex. 23:31; Num. 34:1–12). How far north did the kingdom extend? Where exactly was Dan (Josh. 19:40–48; 1 Kings 5:1–12, 9:10–14; 2 Sam. 24:5–7)? How much of the southern desert was controlled (Josh. 15:1–63; 1 Kings 9:26)? What about the coastal plain, particularly the Philistine cities (1 Kings 2:36–46)? And how long were the nations east of the Jordan kept subservient (1 Kings 11:5–7, 14–25)? Even if the exact borders could be determined, it is not at all clear that Solomon's borders should become the geographic definition of the promised land. Nor does it automatically follow that land promised, received, and lost two thousand years ago can be claimed again on the basis of biblical warrant. The question of borders poses all these questions and more, and we shall need to consider some of these more fully later.

The kingdom built by David and expanded by Solomon was relatively short-lived. When Solomon died, his son Rehoboam was unable to sustain the union between north and south. The northern tribes rejected Rehoboam and selected Jeroboam (1 Kings 12), while Judah and Benjamin remained loyal to Rehoboam. Thus began a period that saw two kingdoms, Israel in the north and Judah in the south. This situation lasted until Israel was destroyed by the Assyrians in 721 B.C.E. and became an Assyrian province. The southern kingdom, Judah, came to an end when the Babylonians destroyed Jerusalem and the temple of Solomon in 587 B.C.E. Persia subsequently took control of the former territories of Israel and Judah. Alexander the Great's empire continued the domination of what had been Israel's land during the fourth century and into the second century B.C.E. The Maccabean Revolt returned independence to Jews in and around Jerusalem for a period of about 130 years (166–37 B.C.E.) before Roman power once again brought an end to freedom. Not until 1948 C.E. did Jews again experience any political authority over the land of Israel.

This brief historical review is intended to demonstrate three things. First, when Israel took possession of the land it had been promised, it did so by displacing those already there. Laying claim to territory necessitated conflict, and keeping territory likewise required force. It was not as if Israel had taken unclaimed land. Quite the contrary, Israel took occupied, settled, titled land, the land of someone else.

Second, only for a brief eighty years did a unified Israel actually rule the promised land. During most of the time before and after David and Solomon, the forebears of the Jews shared the land with other people in a variety of political arrangements with varying degrees of autonomy for the Israelites.

Third, the real or ideal specifications of the land of Israel are difficult to determine because the boundaries were vaguely defined. Thus, even if it were a basis for modern claims, the exact boundaries of David's and Solomon's domain are unknown.

## Land Rights and Responsibilities

The issue of land rights is central to many who live in or are concerned about the Middle East and especially modern Israel. Who has a "right" to be there? How shall land rights be determined? When do interests and needs of a community supersede individual claims? What shall be done to compensate for land taken as a result of war? Who will determine fairness, justice? How long should these concerns remain unsettled?

In most instances, the Bible does not answer these questions directly. It offers a framework, however, that assists those who wish or are constrained to deal with land issues. The biblical perspective is disturbing to many because it places emphasis on land responsibilities rather than land rights. What is done in and with the land and how it is done are the primary concerns, though I will say more about land rights later. Nonetheless, insight can be gained from the biblical traditions bearing on the matters at hand.

Let's begin with how Israel came to occupy the land of Canaan. We have already considered how Israel, over the course of several hundred years, acquired the land through a combination of military victories, treaties, purchases, gradual encroachment and settlement, and default on the part of prior occupants. Between approximately 1200 B.C.E. and 950 B.C.E. the Israelites became the dominant political group in Palestine. In terms of population size and economic power, they probably exceeded other groups still in the land.

53

Certainly these accomplishments warranted a literary epic, but if such an epic ever existed, it has been lost. What we do have in the Bible is an account with a much different tone and purpose. Specific stories celebrate victories or emphasize Israel's accomplishments, but overall the biblical story stresses Israel's responsibility in the land, a responsibility to God, to kin, and to other human beings.

The Bible emphasizes that Israel was *given* the land. Deuteronomy makes this especially clear. Certainly the promise of land is explicit (Deut. 6:23, 7:8, 8:1), but the emphasis is on the utter graciousness of the divine act: The people were without merit (Deut. 7:7, 9:5–6). God brought the people out of Egypt and into a rich land (Deut. 6:10–11, 7:19, 8:7–10). The Lord cared for the people through the wilderness wanderings despite their stubborn rebelliousness (Deut. 8:15–16, 9:6–14). The land was given to Israel because of God's care.

A corollary to God's giving the land to Israel is God's expelling of the prior occupants. It is God, not Israel, who is responsible for removing the Canaanites (Deut. 7:1, 17–21, 8:17–18; Josh. 23:5). While reports of military victory are preserved—where Joshua, for instance, can be said to have taken the land or defeated his enemies (Josh. 11:23, 12:7)—the emphasis remains on God giving the land (Josh. 1:2, 2:9, 24, 8:1). Further, the dispossessing of the Canaanites was not an immoral, capricious act of God but a divine response to their wicked behavior (Deut. 7:23–26, 9:4–5). But God also warned the Israelites that they must not disobey the Almighty as had the Canaanites or they too would be punished (Deut. 8:11–20).

Some, particularly Christians, find the traditions of Israel's entry into Canaan brutal and inhumane; the total destruction and execution of all survivors (Josh. 6:20–21) horrify these individuals. That the carnage resulted from what was understood to be God's command (Deut. 7:2, 16, 24) further offends these persons. Some Christians declare these texts to be typical of the Old Testament as a whole and reject them outright, contending that such a view of God is inferior—indeed inimical—to God as revealed in Jesus of Nazareth.

In response, several points should be noted. First, texts calling for the utter, complete destruction of an enemy are few, and thus it is not fair to contend that these texts are typical.

Second, the reason for the divine command was to keep Israel from being tempted to follow the idolatrous and wicked ways of those being destroyed (Deut. 6:13–15; 7:5–6; Lev. 18:24–25). Those being displaced were understood to be evil and deserving punishment. Thus, this is no wanton killing for killing's sake.

Third, the threat of destruction made and carried out against some of the Canaanites also was made against Israel as well. Whether it be Canaanites or Israelites, disregarding God's way will bring destruction. Indeed, the belief that Jesus was executed in the place of sinners rightly deserving death and the conviction of a Last Judgment are in harmony with the idea of punishment found in some texts of Deuteronomy and Joshua.

Fourth, the fact is that the mass destruction of the population of Canaan did not take place (Josh. 13:1–7, 13, 16:10, 17:12; Judg. 1:27–33, 3:5). Indeed, later generations of Israelites followed the ways of their Canaanite neighbors, and this is cited at the end of Judah's history as part of the reason divine judgment came (2 Kings 23:26–27; Jer. 2:4–37, 5:1–17, 44:1–30).

This leads us into the question of responsibility in relation to the occupation of the land as understood in the Bible. Deuteronomy sets forth the requirement that, to keep the land, the Israelites must obey God's commandments (Deut. 4:25–26, 30:15–20). Other passages make clear the same connection (Josh. 23:6–13; Lev. 18:2–5, 20:22–26, 26:27–33; 1 Kings 9:6–9; Ezek. 33:29).

The rules regulating life in the land were varied, extensive, and detailed. Within the books of Exodus, Leviticus, and Deuteronomy are numerous exhortations and proscriptions aimed at establishing a society pleasing to God. The rules governed ritual, lending and commerce, family matters, warfare, relations between rich and poor, treatment of captives and slaves, and many other aspects of life.

The codes are stated briefly in several places. For instance, there are the well-known Ten Commandments (Ex. 20:1–17; Deut. 5:1–21). The essence of these commandments can be stated as serving the one God loyally and humbly and working for justice and compassion within the human community (Deut. 10:12–22; Micah 6:8). Jesus summed up the law and commandments in much this same way (Matt. 22:34–40; Mark 12:28–34; Luke 10:25–28). Living in accord with these ordinances was central to serving God and crucial to realizing the fullness of life intended by God.

From the biblical perspective, therefore, land rights are quite subordinate to land responsibilities. Israel displaced the former inhabitants of the land because the Canaanites had lived in ways inappropriate before God. Israel had no right to the land as such, though a promise had been given. The divine promise did not entitle Israel to Canaan, but rather called for obedient living in expectation that God would eventually provide a proper inheritance for God's people. Life in the land for Israel was explicitly contingent upon allegiance to God and the faithful, loving establishment of justice and peace within the community.

Many Christians believe, as do some Jews and most Muslims, that ancient Israel lost the land of Canaan because of disobedience before God. Certainly the prophets pronounced such a judgment, first on the northern kingdom (Amos 2:6–16, 9:7–10) and then on all the south (Jer. 5:20—6:30). Some believe that the destruction of Jerusalem in 70 C.E. was God's punishment and brought the final expulsion of the Jews from Canaan and the end to all rightful claims (if any ever existed) on the land. New Testament texts are used to support such contentions (Mark 13:1–13; John 12:37–50, 14:6; Acts 7:51–53; Gal. 3:6—4:7).

This reasoning has two problems. It assumes that (1) at one time Israel was faithful enough to warrant the land, and (2) the point of the Bible is to validate land claims. The Bible contains little if any support for either of these assumptions. As noted previously, Israel was reminded from the outset that it was not its worthiness that prompted God's gracious gift. Moreover, once Israel was in the land, the Bible offers account after account of Israel's disobedience. No attempt is made in the Bible, nor should it be made now, to claim a guarantee to land entitlement on the basis of God's grace.

The message of the passages about the land was that Israel was given stewardship of the land. Occupation and responsible action were inseparably bound. A place was graciously provided for Israel to develop a community that could show the world what God intended for humanity. God's aim was not to make a perpetual land grant but to offer a place for a society to emerge in which God's way was paramount. Land was granted for faithful living before God and with one another.

One other matter should be considered. Many Jews admit that a special land may not be absolutely essential for faithful Jewish living. Nonetheless, it is only in a place of safety, where the social structure can be arranged to allow a rigorous pursuit of the ordinances, that the full possibilities can be realized. This does not mean that Jews must be allowed a land at the expense of others, but it helps to explain the special regard that most Jews hold for modern Israel. The full possibilities for justice can only be realized in a community that controls its own space. The full possibilities of faithfulness before God can only be demonstrated when choices can be made and policies can be set.

From a biblical perspective, life before God always involves human community, and human community always involves specific space (that is, land) where community life can be ordered and experienced. Too many Christians, particularly in the West, disdain or disregard the significance of the reality that we are flesh. They become susceptible to an individualized, privatized, spiritualized form of Christianity that is quite alien to the biblical tradition, with its insistence upon land, incarnation, corporeality, and God's concern for the whole of creation, the world in all its concreteness.

## The Holy Land

People interested in the religious significance of the land refer to Palestine as the Holy Land. Christians, especially, use Holy Land to refer to the places where Jesus was born, raised, ministered, and was crucified and raised from the dead. Thus, for Christians the Holy Land theoretically means Palestine as a whole but actually centers on Bethlehem, Nazareth, the area around the Sea of Galilee, and Jerusalem. Most of the Christian holy sites are located in these places and are revered for their direct association with Jesus. The specific locations of many of the shrines are based only on tradition and date back to Constantine the Great (fourth century C.E.) and a visit to Palestine by Constantine's mother, Queen Helena, after she became a Christian.

Jews also sometimes use the term Holy Land as a reference to Israel. Their term is broader and emphasizes places less significant for Christians like Hebron, Shechem, Jericho, Bethel, Beersheba. When Jews say Holy Land, they think of the whole of the land through which Abraham and Sarah traveled. Sometimes the term Holy Land is used in place of Israel, which can be understood as a political reference. Usually, though, the term is just another way—a more religious way—that Jews, like Christians, refer to the setting of so much of the tradition recounted in the Bible.

The Bible itself, however, practically never uses the term Holy Land. Only in one text, Zechariah 2:12, is the term explicitly employed when referring to Judah as *God's* special inheritance in "the holy land." Otherwise, the references to holy places in the Bible are predominantly to Jerusalem (Isa. 52:1; Neh. 11:1, 18) or Mt. Zion located within Jerusalem (Ps. 2:6, 3:4, 15:1; Joel 3:17). More specifically, the Temple (Ps. 5:7) and its innermost sanctuary (1 Kings 6:16, 8:6) were re-ferred to as "holy." In the same manner, the Tabernacle of the premonarchy period had its special holy place.

Things are considered holy when they are in close contact with God. God's name is holy, and God's Spirit is holy. The

Sabbath is dedicated to God and is therefore holy (Ex. 20:8, 31:14). In God's presence ground may become holy (Ex. 3:5).

The people are holy because God has chosen them especially (Ex. 19:6), but their holiness comes from being set apart by God, not from their own character. In Leviticus, the people of Israel are enjoined to be holy because God is holy. And how are they to do so? By keeping God's commandments (Lev. 19:3 ff; *see* 1 Peter 1:15–16). Detailed ordinances are given by which the people are to live. In the midst of these instructions is the description of a very distinctive institution—the jubilee year. It is the culmination of the commandments by which this chosen people would demonstrate holiness.

The jubilee year is to occur every fifty years as a Sabbath for seven "weeks of years" (Lev. 25:8). The most distinctive feature of the jubilee year is that property originally received at the distribution of the land when Israel entered Canaan reverts to the family to whom it was first given (Lev. 25:13), thereby ensuring that no family can fall into perpetual servitude. If property is lost as payment of debt, it is returned at the jubilee (Lev. 25:28, 31). Those who sell themselves or their children into slavery in payment of debts will be released (Lev. 25:41).

The basis for this unique institution is this: the land was never understood as belonging to Israel at all. It *belonged* to God! All are dependent upon God's graciousness and are allowed to use the land at God's pleasure. Thus, all are to have compassion for one another, to love and care for neighbors, to be holy as God is holy. God's land is only loaned to them, and every fifty years there is a radical reminder of this God-defined arrangement.

There is no clear evidence that the year of jubilee was actually observed. Jeremiah contains a record of something like it being tried, but major differences from the Levitical jubilee existed in the aborted effort (Jer. 34:1ff). Nonetheless, the ideal is clear. Because God owns the land, the people of Israel are never more than caretakers. They are not free to do whatever they wish in the land because, in the end, it is not theirs. At the same time, they are not less than caretakers, either, because the land is entrusted to them for safekeeping. They are to deal with one another justly. They are to act responsibly and strive to be the holy people they were chosen to be.

When we refer to Israel or Palestine as the Holy Land, we would do well to remember that the biblical perspective is much more concerned with the people in that land and their faithful stewardship of it than the land itself. The significance of all things "holy" is that they point to the source of all holiness: God, the Holy One of Israel. Apart from God nothing is holy. Christians during the Crusades did a disservice to God when they massacred countless "unbelievers," "infidels," in their misconceived effort to rescue the Holy Land. The land can be holy only if the people in it honor God's way. The holiness does not reside in the land but in the God to whom the land belongs and before whom all are to seek to live justly, honorably, and compassionately.

## God's Land

The modern country of Israel is called in Hebrew *eretz Yisrael*, literally "the land of Israel." The word *eretz* can designate several things: from a specific territory such as "the land of your sojournings" (Gen. 28:4; Ex. 6:4) or "the land of the Philistines" (Gen. 21:32, 34; Ex. 13:17) to "earth" as parallel with "heaven" (Gen. 24:3). Sometimes *eretz* means "ground," as when something or someone falls to the ground (2 Sam. 2:22, 14:11; 2 Kings 10:10). Despite contemporary usage, *eretz Yisrael*, in the sense of being the whole territory, occurs rather infrequently (1 Sam. 13:19; Ezek. 40:2, 47:18; 1 Chron. 22:2; 2 Chron. 2:17, 34:7). Another Hebrew word *adamah* also can be translated "land." But *adamah* generally means "dirt" (1 Sam. 4:12; Isa. 45:9), "cultivated land" as opposed to wilderness (Gen. 2:5, 47:23).

The multiple meanings of *eretz* lead to another insight: God not only owns the land; God also creates the earth. By opening as it does, the Bible presents an affirmation with far-reaching

consequences. In the first chapter of Genesis, God alone creates the earth and then sets about to make it a good place for
all living things. Humankind is created in God's very image
(Gen. 1:26–27), and is given authority over and responsibility
for keeping all the earth (Gen. 1:28–30). In the most fundamental way, then, the earth belongs to the God of Israel. Thus,
human beings are earth-keepers responsible to God the earth's
Creator.

From a biblical perspective, any discussion of land finally
must acknowledge divine ownership and dominion. Human
land claims are always secondary, derived, conditional.
Human owners and occupants come and go, but God remains; the land—indeed the whole earth—is God's. The only
totally adequate way to refer to particular land and to the
whole of the earth is to call it God's land.

Of course, in our modern world many scorn the idea that
God has created and thereby rightly claims the earth as
divine territory and domain. To take the biblical perspective,
however, is to affirm this very idea. From this point of view,
human responsibility is recognized as awesome, and human
claims of ownership are never seen as absolute. Scripture is
clear that God intends blessing. The inhabitants of earth
become the agents and participants of God's stewardship of
God's land as earth-keepers. Activities and claims that run
counter to this basic affirmation are thus suspect for those
who wish to be guided by the Bible.

A New Heaven and a New Earth

Both Jewish and Christian traditions contain the hope for a
new world, a new heaven and a new earth, which God will
create to replace our existing earth with all of its pain and
injustice. This visionary or eschatological (dealing with the
end of the world) view is not dominant, but it is persistent
and powerful. Within the Bible and in each generation subsequent to it, this vision was for some people the source of
encouragement to endure, and was the basis for a hope that

had little concrete reality in their own lives. What can we learn from this understanding of land?

The vision is rooted in the prophetic view of God's judgment and restoration of the people and the land. The imagery used by the prophets included the shaking of the heavens and the earth as God punished iniquity (Amos 9:5–6; Joel 3:16). Similarly, God's forgiveness will bring blessing on the land in the form of abundant crops and lush vegetation (Amos 9:13–15; Joel 3:18). Likewise, the human community will be made whole; injustice will be banished and injuries healed (Zeph. 3:14–20; Hos. 14:4–7; Isa. 25:6–8). A peaceful kingdom will be established where God's way prevails (Isa. 11:1–9, 65:17–25).

This imagery probably was not intended to be taken literally but was poetic exaggeration aimed at expressing the seriousness of judgment and the grandeur of restoration. As the tradition developed, however, some understood the language in a more direct manner: a new heaven and a new earth would replace the worn-out, corrupted world of present experience (Isa. 66:22; 2 Peter 3:10, 13; Rev. 21:1–4). In literature outside the Bible, this relatively infrequently found viewpoint was developed extensively. But it is this apocalyptic vision of the end of the world that many mistakenly believe is standard in the Bible.

Whether one understands the imagery to be literal or not, it is important to recognize that a place, a land, is essential to the realization of God's ways. Punishment is described in terms of earthly experience: drought, pestilence, war, death. Restoration or forgiveness is expressed in equally concrete terms: rescue from danger, release of prisoners, healing of disease, peace, and abundant crops. The Bible seems not to recognize disembodied punishment or salvation. To those who wrote the Bible, it was simply inconceivable that there could be no place of God's choosing, no Jerusalem, no land. Radical renewal might be necessary—even the creation of a new heaven, a new earth, a new Jerusalem—but God's interaction with humanity could only be expressed in terms of concrete, material existence. We should hesitate to forsake this under-standing too quickly even though the imagery does not fit readily into our contemporary world view. After all, it is not much stranger than the insistence among Christians that the presence of Jesus is known in the sharing of bread and the fruit of the vine.

## Concluding Reflection

The biblical perspectives we have explored here are varied. The importance of land, the land, cannot be denied. God's promise of land and occupation of the land constitute a ma-jor theme in the narrative from Genesis through Joshua. The necessity of a space, a land, for the faithful following of God's ways—with accompanying blessing and punishment—is made clear in numerous passages. The insistence that it is God alone who can give land is based on the radical recogni-tion that the land—all the land, the earth—finally belongs only to God. And God may even provide a new earth and a new heaven if need be so that human community and life may reach the fullness that God wills.

To disregard this rich and diverse tradition can only be done by ignoring or abandoning the Bible. For some who disregard the tradition of land, this leads to rejecting especially the Hebrew Scriptures, the Old Testament, as either inadequate, inferior, or erroneous. Many Christians take this course and insist on a spiritual understanding that claims to be universal and free of such mundane issues as land. Unfortunately, his-torically speaking, these same Christians have all too often been concerned with imposing their views on and governing over as many others as possible. The proper response to the concreteness of the Bible is neither a falsely literal biblicism nor an arrogantly disdainful modernism. Rather, those who seek to adopt the biblical perspective will listen carefully to the tradition, seeking to discern how it may instruct us amid the complex realities of our contemporary world. This may not always be easy, but is critical and excitingly engaging.

## For Further Reading

Brueggemann, Walter. *The Land: Place as Gift, Promise, and Challenge in Biblical Faith*. Minneapolis: Fortress, 1977.

Davies, W. D. *The Gospel and the Land*. Berkeley: University of California Press, 1974.

Evans, Bernard F. and Gregory D. Cusack, eds. *Theology of the Land*. Collegeville, Minn.: Liturgical Press, 1987.

Heschel, Abraham Joshua. *Israel: An Echo of Eternity*. New York: Farrar, Straus & Giroux, 1987.

Lilburne, Geoffrey R. *A Sense of Place: A Christian Theology of the Land*. Nashville: Abingdon Press, 1989.

# 4 | God's Way and Israel: Theological Reflections on a Particular Land

For Reformed Christians, the activities of governments and societies are always subject to scrutiny and criticism. The starting point for any analysis is the conviction that God as Creator and Ruler has the final authority and is the ultimate judge. All human behavior is to be measured against God's way, God's norm. Such a theological assertion finds support within the Bible but is also based on creedal statements developed by the church. For Reformed Christians, theology—as well as the Bible—supplies important insights by which to assess present reality.

Over the centuries, a number of theological statements concerning Israel have been developed by Christians. Many concern biblical Israel or use the term Israel to refer to the church as the continuation of God's people. Many Christians have uncritically used these theological statements as a basis for understanding and relating to the modern nation Israel. Some Christians have been unreservedly pro-Israel, assuming the creation of modern Israel has indisputable religious significance. Other Christians, drawing upon biblical denunciations of ancient Israel by the prophets or the apostles, have taken an equally solid stance against modern Israel, rejecting any positive theological understanding for fear of incorrectly validating Israel or its politics.

To reflect on the importance of land and to concentrate particularly on Israel, we must consider some of the theological assumptions that many Christians (and others as well) draw upon in relation to this topic. Many of their working suppositions are strongly held and filled with emotion or religious convictions. For some, it will be threatening and disturbing for their assertions to be challenged or disputed. Nevertheless, clarification is important, and in many instances new understandings need to replace previously held views.

In light of what we know about the peoples of Israel, the historical circumstances of the nation, and the biblical tradition, my goal in this chapter is to consider and reformulate a number of theological statements often heard in discussions about modern Israel and land. Errors in opinion are usually relatively easy to correct, but much more important and difficult to counter are convictions that need reconsideration in view of changed conditions. Reformed Christians believe that God's Spirit is always at work, bringing new insight and new reality to light. With this in mind, I will seek to shape a new understanding of how God and Israel are related and what this may mean with respect to land.

## Is Israel "Israel"?

When we start thinking about modern Israel, several beliefs should be recognized and avoided. The first one equates the modern entity with Israel, the people mentioned in the Bible. There is no direct, obvious, unassailable way to equate the two distinct historical realities.

Modern Israel was so named with the deliberate intention of claiming for itself the legacy of ancient Israel, the rightful reconstitution in Palestine of a long-absent people. Some Jews may actually be able to trace their lineage back to ancient Israel, though this is highly unlikely. But modern Israel is a new geopolitical organization fashioned for the most part in the past fifty years. That it is situated on land once occupied by another Israel is true, but that does not mean that when we read Israel in the Bible we should automatically and rightly think of modern Israel as the continuation of the ancient people. It is fair to say that modern Israel was created to provide haven for Jews and a place where Judaism could be lived without hindrance.

Judaism, it should be remembered, developed parallel to Christianity during the second and third centuries of the Common Era. Judaism emerged after the fall of Jerusalem (70 C.E.) largely as a continuation and development of the practices of a group known as the Pharisees. Judaism was based in part on the Bible, but even more upon traditions now preserved in the Talmud. At the time, Judaism took a form that can be regarded as the precursor of contemporary Judaism. But Jews were not allowed to live in Jerusalem and only in a few scattered places elsewhere in Palestine (mainly in the Galilee). Jews remembered Jerusalem across the centuries as the ancient center of a people from whom they were descended and as a place of unique holiness. But modern Israel is a new creation. It is a place for Jews and for the expression of Judaism, but it is not the source of Judaism.

Israel is not biblical Israel, and any rights held by biblical Israel do not belong to modern Israel. The promises and the relationship with God claimed by biblical Israel are now part of the legacy of both Judaism and Christianity. When we read the Bible, we must be quite clear that its Israel is not the modern nation.

## Is the Church "Israel"?

If modern Israel is not to be equated with biblical Israel, what about the church? Did not the church become the "new Israel"? Didn't the Jews reject Jesus and in return receive the punishment and rejection of God? The church long taught this, and forcible expulsions, oppression, and discrimination against Jews resulted. But is it true that the church is the new Israel?

This position has come under attack during the past thirty years. The Holocaust provided stark evidence that the church had nourished anti-Semitism over several centuries. Supersessionism is the idea that Christianity replaced Judaism, with the church assuming the place of Israel in God's eyes. In

Western Christianity, such a view was used by Hitler and his propagandists to justify the "final solution," the attempted eradication of all European Jews (and if Hitler had won, of all Jews). Many Christians cooperated, directly and indirectly, in the Holocaust. Many Christians turned a deaf ear to Jewish cries for help. And while Eastern Christians are quick to deny any involvement in the destruction of European Jewry, their history is stamped by a virulent anti-Jewish attitude, both before and after the founding of modern Israel. Supersessionism lies at the root of this hostility.

Can God have intended Christians to murder Jews? Does the continued existence of Judaism, despite centuries of persecution at the hands of Christians, Muslims, and others, not suggest that God still cares for Jews? Could it be that the church, after it became the state religion under Constantine in 324 C.E., misappropriated a tradition that had been cast in an era of conflict between Christians and Jews (100–200 C.E.)? Many contemporary Christians, on the basis of such questions, have urged a serious and immediate reconsideration of the church's position on Jews and Judaism.

Much in the same way that it is wrong to equate modern Israel with ancient, biblical Israel, so it is not accurate to understand the church as the simple continuation of ancient Israel. Perhaps the church shares with Judaism a relationship to biblical Israel, but the church alone is not God's Israel. Divine promises to ancient Israel must now be heard in light of two realities: the emergence of both Judaism and Christianity. However Christians may think and talk about their biblical heritage, they cannot assume to own it all by themselves. Two vital communities, Judaism and Christianity, claim direct descent from those who lived by and preserved the biblical stories; a third, Islam, treasures the tradition as well.

## Is God Gathering "Israel"?

Many Christians embrace the belief that the creation of modern Israel is the "fulfillment of prophecy." This idea is certainly rooted in Scripture and a number of texts can be brought forward to prove the position. Some Jews also use the Bible in this way to validate the existence of modern Israel. It is important to realize that this understanding is based upon an interpretation of the texts usually guided by theological convictions that are not clearly and unmistakably biblical.

The simplest version of the argument among Christians is that all the words of the prophets must be fulfilled because the prophets were predicting the future. Some prophecies have been fulfilled, but many have not. Among the latter is the prediction that at the end of time or at the beginning of the messianic age, the people of Israel—scattered abroad when their nation was destroyed as punishment from God—will be gathered and returned to their former land. Sometimes in this view, the return is seen as the beginning of a time when Jews will be converted to Christianity or at least will acknowledge that Jesus is Messiah. For others, the ingathering of Jews is simply a sign of the end time, when Christians will be delivered from this evil world before final judgment falls on the nations.

On the surface, the argument is persuasive if the texts in question are read according to the presupposed theology. But a number of criticisms may rightly be lodged against this interpretation. First, the texts are taken out of their literary and historical contexts and understood as predictions, when in fact they were words of accusation and hope directed to particular audiences of real people. These were not mysterious words that would only be understood thousands of years after they were uttered. The whole notion is based on a misunderstanding of the character and intention of the biblical prophets and their work.

Second, how does anyone know what has or has not been fulfilled? A biblical vision certainly exists of a time when all of God's people gather to praise God and live in peace and harmony, but can the establishment of modern Israel be the fulfillment of this grand vision?

To cite but one passage generally considered to address such a hope, Ezekiel 47 speaks of a new temple with a stream flowing from it that waters the whole land. The Dead Sea becomes fresh water; an abundance of life blossoms through-out the land. Extensive borders are described and within them land is reallocated according to the ancient tribal boundaries. Aliens within Israel will be given land as well. Now, this is a beautiful vision, but it certainly does not describe modern Israel. Of course, one can interpret the passage nonliterally and talk about how modern Israel has brought life to the desert through irrigation and cultivation, but such a figurative reading of the text leaves no logical basis for interpreting the text or Israel as a literal fulfillment of prophetic vision.

Finally, this argument ignores the fact that many of the texts can be understood to be fulfilled (if one must) by the return of the exiles from Babylon in 538 B.C.E. and the next several years. Certainly, some people in restored Jerusalem during the time of Haggai and Zechariah understood them-selves in light of Isaiah's words and those of such prophets as Jeremiah and Ezekiel. To disregard the context in which these words were proclaimed, heard, and gathered is to do them damage.

Much more could be said in criticism of this position, which is vigorously advocated by some Christians known as "dispensationalists" and others known as "premillennialists." (See "For Further Reading.") The fundamental error, however, is to read texts intended to engender hope and consolation too literally. The words were intended to assure God's people of ongoing divine care and compassion. They may help us articulate a vision, but they do not constitute a deterministic program we can use to predict God's time.

Is Israel God's Creation?

Some Christians and Jews attribute modern Israel's cre-ation to the hand of God, a direct act of God. Other Chris-tians, Jews, and Muslims vehemently denounce such a view for a variety of reasons. What are we to make of this? Is it correct to say that modern Israel was created by God?

From a Christian perspective, it seems that the possibility of grave error resides in both positions. To say Israel is the result of divine intervention is to invite such unsupportable corollaries as: (1) God ordained the Holocaust to make Jews return to Palestine, or (2) God willed the suffering of hundreds of thousands of Palestinian Christians and Muslims who have been displaced by the creation of Israel. On the other hand, to say God had nothing whatsoever to do with the establishment of modern Israel, to argue that human politics alone gave rise to the Jewish state, is to suggest that (1) God has no interest or influence in world history, and (2) God is indifferent to human struggle and pain. Reformed Christians cannot settle for positions ascribing the formation of Israel simply to God or denying that the creation of a Jewish state has any religious significance whatsoever.

The struggle to create a modern Israel is clearly a very human history. Political and military actions by Muslims, Christians, and Jews were very real. Nations were involved; the United Nations acted. Reformed Christians believe that God's purpose is somehow assisted and resisted through such human efforts. Thus it would be wrong to say that no religious significance accompanied the momentous establishment of modern Israel. The nation was founded, at least in part, because of the dire circumstances in which Jews had fallen at the hands of Europeans who characterized themselves as Christians. For many Jews, the haven that became Israel was their only hope for survival. Certainly this has religious significance.

Because Reformed Christians believe that God does have a stake in what human beings do, they can also insist that part of the importance of Israel rests in how Israel lives among its neighbors. In the ambiguity of human existence, the creation of Israel was marked by injustice for some while providing deliverance for others. When Jews moved in, Palestinians had to move over or get out; inequities have occurred. While all

71

parties involved can claim their share of atrocities, both as perpetrators and victims, it remains the burden of the government of Israel to act in a responsible and just manner for all within its borders. The religious significance of Israel in the longer term will be determined by how the rich ethical teaching of Judaism is embodied by the only state calling itself Jewish. Many Jews think it unfair to be judged by more rigorous norms than other nations, but Israel has set its own standard by declaring itself a Jewish state. Reformed Christians hope Israel will live by those high ideals.

One final word of warning is necessary about the issue of how to understand the fact of Israel's existence. Christians have no basis on which to claim moral superiority or divine destiny. The nations they inhabit, including the United States, have very ambiguous human origins. Violence and injustice can be found in all national histories. While Israel may warrant criticism on occasion, the misdeeds and failings of other nations should not be overlooked. Since Reformed Christians do criticize the government of Israel, they should also consider and comment upon the records of the surrounding Arab nations, many of which are autocratic. Some may believe it too much to say God created Israel, but let no one say that Israel doesn't matter to God or that Israel's life as a nation is illegitimate. Israel does exist and has provided much good for many—even though there are clearly wrongs that should be corrected. God is as concerned for Israel as for each of the other nations of the world.

## Is Israel Spiritually Significant?

Christians are prone to adopt yet another position, expressing a preference for things that are "spiritual" and "universal" over things that are "material" and "particular." Christianity long has had a tendency to take pride in being a faith that values the "universal" over the "particular." The universal significance of Christ, for instance, is more important for many than the particular life of Jesus. Since the very beginning of Christianity, there have been those who sought to disprove or at least de-emphasize the material character of Jesus, the realness of his humanity in all of its particularity. In this viewpoint, Jesus as the divine, spiritual manifestation of God was what was really important.

The consequences of this error are wide-reaching. Rather than understand God's blessings in any way as earthly and material, Christians have often characterized them as heavenly and spiritual. Rather than address and redress the wrongs of this world, some have encouraged a passive acceptance of tyranny in expectation of an other-worldly existence of plenty and painlessness. Material existence has too often been characterized as finite, futile, and essentially sinful. Spiritual existence is touted as superior in every way, and it requires a fundamental rejection of material reality.

When one then asks about the spiritual significance of Israel, this is to some a loaded question. Undoubtedly, many Christians do not believe that modern Israel has spiritual significance. They believe that Judaism is at worst a Godless perversion of the truth and at best of no more importance than any other human (that is, pagan) religious system. After all, they argue, Judaism concentrates on particulars rather than universals. By its insistence on ethnicity guarded by restricted interaction with others, it misses universal truth entirely or at best distorts it. Some Christians think that by concentrating on fulfilling 613 specific rules, Jews have missed the universal aim of the law. Christian attitudes of disdain and superiority with respect to Jews are often the real logic that guides this negative perception.

Does Israel have spiritual significance? Yes. But this answer cannot be understood to deny or disregard the material significance of Israel. It is, above all, a real, concrete, material state in a particular, geographically specific place in this world. Because it is real and of this world, it is not perfect. Biblical tradition is rooted in the lives of specific people in particular communities. Loving God and loving neighbor cannot be realized in the abstract. Thus, for those Jews who wish to live out their understanding of obedience to God in the fullest possible way, a specific place is required. Despite the numerous difficulties, it is only in the "promised land," according to the Torah, that *all* the commandments can be obeyed. Without security and some level of autonomy in Palestine, Jewish culture cannot be realized fully. The state of Israel, therefore, does have spiritual significance, at least for Jews.

It is important, however, to go further because for Christians ancient Israel was a "particular" that pointed beyond itself to "universals." Ancient Israel was intended, among other things, to provide a model of God's way for the world. God's Torah (teaching) was entrusted to ancient Israel so that humanity could understand how to live together. How well ancient Israel succeeded in this task is not the question here, but Jews and Christians, for the most part, recognize this function as part of ancient Israel's calling. Thus, as a particular nation among nations, ancient Israel had a role that went beyond that of others.

Modern Israel, insofar as it attempts to be a Jewish state, shares some of the same burden and blessing of ancient Israel. By seeking to enable Jews and the non-Jews in their midst to live in accordance with God's way, some contend that the nation points beyond itself. It is not only a nation like other nations, but it also has accepted an additional objective, namely that of demonstrating in this concrete, real world the spiritual reality of God's desire that human beings live in ways that honor their Creator and respect one another. By claiming what is at least in part a religious dimension, some see modern Israel seeking to point beyond itself, to be a light for others, to demonstrate spiritual significance in a this-world setting.

## Is Israel God's Chosen?

Another claim we must consider is the notion that Israel is a "chosen people." Some Christians take such an idea to mean that modern Israel is a nation of divine destiny. Others denounce any notion that only one people or one nation can be "chosen." Still other Christians contend the church is now the "chosen people" and thus "chosenness" has become less particular, less ethnic, and certainly nonmaterialistic.

To speak of Israel, ancient or modern, as chosen by God must be done with great care. Certainly numerous biblical texts speak of ancient Israel as chosen. Those same texts, however, make it absolutely clear that being chosen was not based on intrinsic superiority of any kind. Being chosen simply meant that ancient Israel was given a task and was held accountable. In somewhat the same way, it is permissible to speak of the church as chosen.

What is most interesting, however, is that the Ruler of the universe decided to relate to humanity through the medium of a very particular people. Israel was chosen to be the people–nation with which God would demonstrate divine compassion, judgment, deliverance, and all the rest. Jesus was born a Jew. The Bible presents God as one who has made commitments to a particular, worldly company and has known in detail the frailties of humankind. The God of heaven and earth, at least as far as the Bible is concerned, is not known in some abstract way. Rather than Unmoved Mover or Ground of Being, God has a name and has interacted with people from time immemorial as one who chooses and makes commitments.

It is not right to say modern Israel has been chosen by God in some way that other nations have not. It is correct, however, to say that, insofar as God is known by any, it is by God's choice. To the degree that any nation lives with a sense of being chosen by God, it can only mean that the nation is under obligation to love God and neighbor in such a way that others are directed to God. In this sense, every nation and no nation may be chosen.

What seems incredible in the modern world is that human beings can matter so much to God and that the Creator of all would risk becoming involved with any particular group as a way to reach out to all. Many modern people cannot fathom how that could work, so they conclude it cannot be what God has done. They insist that particular historical events and nations are simply the result of chance or causation of some sort and thus have no real value or meaning. Biblical tradition keeps insisting, however, that God is at work in and with these events and peoples.

Modern Israel is not chosen by God as a nation above nations. At the same time, however, modern Israel is chosen by God as a particular place where the divine claims on human life can be made concrete and visible. Also chosen in this sense is every nation where Jew and Christian dwell. Whether modern Israel has been chosen for anything more, only history will tell, for it is in history that God brings life and judgment to nations.

## Is Israel's Land God-given?

Some contemporary Christians and Jews assume that Israel possesses its land by divine action. This erroneous view is defended by references to promises made by God to Abraham and Sarah, their progeny, and later to David. All the land traversed by Abraham and Sarah during their sojourn in Canaan, so the argument goes, is intended by God to belong to modern Israel. Biblical names displace modern names. Samaria and Judea are used instead of Jordan or West Bank. Nablus is called Shechem. The territory of ancient Israel is claimed as the God-given land, to be held and governed by modern Israel.

This position has several problems. First, its proponents often cite a long list of biblical passages in support of their claims. These passages, however, fall into three categories: (1) texts which were fulfilled with the entry of ancient Israel into the land (Genesis, Deuteronomy and Joshua); (2) texts fulfilled by the return from the Babylonian exile (for example, passages from Isaiah, Jeremiah, Haggai, and Zechariah); and (3) passages referring to the end time or the last days, texts that can only be fulfilled by the appearance of a new heaven and new earth (for example, certain passages from Isaiah,

Ezekiel, Joel, and Daniel). None of these passages support land claims now! The authority of such claims, if any ever existed, either was used thousands of years ago or must await a new age. Because God may have granted land in the past does not mean that modern Israel has a legal justification for occupying the land now.

The founders of modern Israel recognized this. Their efforts to buy land in Palestine, beginning in the last decades of the nineteenth century and continuing to the establishment of the current nation, is clear testimony to their understanding. The tireless political activity aimed at creating the nation also signals a realistic understanding of the ways of the world. Those who dreamed of a Jewish haven, a new Jewish state, may have finally decided that Jerusalem and the surrounding area were the most appropriate area, but they knew that they could not claim the land on the basis of prior ownership. For the religious, such claims based on the Bible may make some sense, but in courts of law and in circles where human justice counts, such divine right to land is insufficient.

Israel does have legal right to much of its land. It was granted by the United Nations at the time of partition. Whether popular or not, a decision was made that allowed a new nation to be born with all the rights of nationhood. A territory was defined, and Israel assumed responsibility for defending its borders and citizens from attack—a task it has effectively exercised.

For many years most Muslims and many Christians denounced or ignored the action of the United Nations. While it is understandable that the Arab nations and the displaced Palestinians deeply resent an action by other nations that granted Israel the right to be established on what they consider Arab land, the reality nonetheless is that the United Nations did just that. So far as the international community is concerned, Israel is legal and has territorial rights. The irony is that this same international community offers the best hope for justice for the region's refugees and some resolution of the continuing dispute over borders. The United

Nations has repeatedly asked for all parties to address these issues. In 1993, Israel and the Palestinians took the first steps toward a political solution, and other Arab entities moved toward a honorable peace settlement that recognizes Israel's right of secure borders.

To repeat, the claim of some Jews and Christians that the occupied territories, especially Samaria and Judea or the West Bank, belong to Israel because the Bible says so has absolutely no legal weight within the international community. It is nonetheless of interest within certain religious communities and thus warrants further comment.

Claims that the land was given by God raise two important issues. First is the matter of divine promises. If God promised the land to the offspring of Sarah and Abraham, then the trustworthiness of God is on the line. God's promises must be kept or God is diminished. At one level it can be said, as was noted earlier, that the interpretation of the texts is crucial because some argue that the promises of land and a return to land were kept in ancient Israel's history or can only be kept at the end of time. Some, particularly Christians, want to argue that modern Israel's emergence is a sign of the last days. If so, then using the argument to justify the legality of territorial claims is rather moot. What's more, at this literalistic level, Christians and Muslims should also have a share in the land since they too are descendants of Abraham.

At a more important level, God's trustworthiness does not depend upon the vicissitudes of human politics. God was with Abraham and Sarah before they went forth. God was with Israel in the wilderness, during the Exile, and throughout the Diaspora. God can be believed whether Jews return to the land occupied by ancient Israel or not, and many Jews willingly and eloquently attest to this. God's honor is not at risk in this discussion.

The second issue raised by claims of God-given land concerns assumptions that God is involved in the affairs of human history and whether a particular place is required for the full expression of Judaism. Few people of faith argue that

God is uncaring or uninvolved in human history, but wide disagreements exist over how God is engaged in these events. But does Judaism require a specific place in which to live out religious conviction? Jerusalem has long had special significance to Jews, and certain commandments can only be fulfilled there. Nonetheless, Judaism does not require the establishment or continuation of modern Israel for its existence or continuation, although the renewed commitment and hope that modern Israel has brought to countless Jews should not be denied or underestimated.

What is required for any person of faith is a concrete place in a real world where decision is called for and righteousness and justice can be practiced. To affirm this is to acknowledge the significance of a land promise without using it to justify political claims for autonomy over particular territory by any group. It is to insist that every group must be secure in its practice of religion and in the opportunity for fulfilling life. If there is God-given land, it is earth, a consideration that will be treated more fully in the concluding chapter.

## Interpretation as a Theological Task

As frequently noted in the preceding pages, theological assertions have arisen over the centuries to help people understand who God is and how God engages humankind. Because of the prominence of Israel in biblical tradition and the tension known in the first two centuries of Christianity between Jews and the church, many formulations appeared to explain how such matters fit within God's purposes. For centuries many of these theological ideas were assumed as correct by Christians while they were deeply offensive and literally harmful to Jews.

Reformed Christians believe that each new generation is given the task of listening again to its tradition and fashioning appropriate interpretation in light of current reality. God has brought about surprising, unexpected, humanly inexplicable things in the past and may well do so again. Old views may need to be refashioned or even discarded. Continuity is provided in the constancy of God's love, but always a new thing may appear.

In the late twentieth century, events such as the murder of six million European Jews and the establishment of modern Israel in a predominantly Arab region require a reconsideration of theological understanding. The task of interpretation is far from complete, but a start has been made. However Israel (with all the possible nuances of that term) is to be understood finally, Reformed Christians contend that God's promises are sure, God's commitments are real, and God's intentions for justice and peace remain unqualified. Good theology will emerge as historical reality and biblical witness to assist people of faith in once again fashioning proper response to God's way.

*For Further Reading*

On the relation of Christians with Jews:

*A Theological Understanding of the Relationship Between Christians and Jews.* Louisville, Ky.: Office of the General Assembly, the Presbyterian Church (U.S.A.), 1987.

*The Theology of the Churches and the Jewish People.* New York: World Council of Churches. WCC Publications, 1988.

Falk, Randall M. *Jews and Christians: A Troubled Family.* Nashville: Abingdon Press, 1990.

Gager, John G. *The Origins of Anti-Semitism.* New York: Oxford University Press, 1983.

Ruether, Rosemary R. *Faith and Fratricide—The Theological Roots of Anti-Semitism.* San Francisco: Seabury Press, 1974.

On dispensationalism and premillennialism:

*Eschatology. The Doctrine of Last Things.* Materials Distribution Center, the Presbyterian Church in the United States, 1978.

Ariel, Yaakov. *On Behalf of Israel: American Fundamentalist Atti-*

*tudes Toward Jews, Judaism, and Zionism, 1865–1945.* Brooklyn: Carlson Press, 1991.

Cox, William E. *An Examination of Dispensationalism.* Philadelphia: Presbyterian and Reformed Publishing House, 1963.

Weber, Timothy P. *Living in the Shadow of the Second Coming: American Premillennialism, 1875–1982.* Chicago: University of Chicago Press, 1987.

On the place of Jerusalem and Israel for Jews:

Heschel, Abraham Joshua. *Israel: An Echo of Eternity.* New York: Farrar, Straus and Giroux, 1987.

Hoffman, Lawrence A. *The Land of Israel: Jewish Perspectives.* South Bend, Ind.: University of Notre Dame, 1986.

Rudin, James A. *Israel for Christians.* Minneapolis: Fortress Press, 1983.

# 5 | A Guiding Vision: A Call to Be Earth-keepers

In light of the preceding historical, biblical, and theological review, the final task is to articulate some general conclusions. Is there a guiding vision that emerges from this discussion to give direction when disputes over land and land use occur? What can we learn from this case study of modern Israel that will be helpful in other situations? Assuming that a guiding vision indeed emerges, to whom is it addressed and toward what goal? This concluding chapter will explore these questions.

But first, a word about guiding visions, which are often a little fuzzy around the edges. Some would prefer detailed plans, concrete blueprints, absolute answers. Ambiguity is difficult to tolerate in the best of circumstances and becomes quite problematic in bad situations. Nonetheless, I will present a guiding vision, with all the difficulties of doing so. I offer no guarantees, no foolproof schemes.

Nonetheless, a guiding vision can help to identify false claims as well as things that don't ring true or sit well in light of the vision. A guiding vision can inspire continued struggle even against great odds and keep those who embrace the vision from being satisfied with substitutes. A guiding vision should spark dissatisfaction with injustice and inequity while beckoning toward a reality that is not yet but will surely be. Those who have been grasped by a guiding vision may become the engineers, the builders, the problem solvers needed for a particular situation. But, without a guiding vision, most often nothing happens to overcome the power of inertia.

I will present a vision here, an ideal toward which to work. The vision is not the construction of any one group or any one religion. The vision is intended to unite, not divide. Finally, the guiding vision presented here requires human participation. The guiding vision cannot and will not be imposed by God or anyone else. Human beings must accept responsibility and become earth-keepers if the vision is ever to become reality. This guiding vision entails no new call, but now the circumstances of earth and all that it sustains are such that an imperative is needed. Earth-keepers guided by a vision fixed on God and God's way are the final concern of this book.

## The Basic Premise: God the Creator

The guiding vision is this: God, the only legitimate land owner, has placed humankind in garden-earth and expects us to be earth-keepers who will enjoy and maintain the earth in order that all may know God's peace (shalom) that is characterized by justice and equity for all. With this vision, earth-keepers seek to follow God's way and find in the vision a source of encouragement and renewal.

Basic to the guiding vision is the conviction that God is the Creator of all that is. As the Creator, God has rightful claim on earth, a claim that no human individual or government can invalidate. Planet Earth belongs to God. As Creator, God can and has set the rules and intends that human beings will respect and live within them. Earth is to be responsibly tended as a luxurious garden for the benefit of the whole human family. Earth is not to be exploited by or for anyone. Earth, God's good land, has been placed in human hands by a loving Creator who desires that all live in harmony and prosperity—that is, in shalom, peace.

This is clearly a vision based upon faith. No one can prove the truth of this vision. No one can demonstrate God's reality to the satisfaction of the skeptical or cynical. Nonetheless, those who believe that God has created earth and all that is in it have been given a vision of how to live. Christians share this vision with others, particularly with Jews and Muslims. To be sure, variations of specifics exist, but the fundamental agreement on the vision is most important. Earth-keepers do not own the vision. Rather, they are owned by it. The guiding vision is simple enough, at least to see if not to follow. This vision has numerous implications, however, and we will now examine them.

## A Purposeful Creation

In antiquity, no one questioned whether there was God or whether God was the Creator. There were numerous rivals to the title of "creator," but human beings unquestioningly assumed that the Creator was a deity not to be confused with the creatures fashioned by divine power. Among religious traditions, disputes occurred over which "God" was Creator God, but no debate about the reality of a Creator God.

Belief that God exists and that God is Creator is not so automatic anymore. In rejecting rampant superstition and the spiritual and mental slavery that often accompanied it, belief in God has also been cast aside in some cases. While perhaps not denying divine reality altogether, many people in the industrialized nations go about their daily lives as if no God existed. Decisions, values, goals, relationships—life is lived without any specific reference to God. Practically speaking, God does not exist for many such people.

As already noted, the existence of God cannot be proved conclusively. No absolutely convincing argument can be made, nor will a logical syllogism win the day. It may help to press people to admit where their reason or experience necessarily must give way to premise or supposition. After all, premise and supposition are other words for beliefs, for those unprovable assumptions about life. Still, the reality of God cannot be proved, only believed and allowed to shape life.

Christians, Jews, and Muslims share the conviction that God created earth purposefully. Creation was not an accident; God determined to create the universe and to assign its care to humankind. Attempts to ascribe creation to some lesser deity or simply to a cosmic accident have regularly been rejected in favor of reaffirming that God responsibly and intentionally created all that is.

Those who self-consciously seek to be guided by the vision of God and God's way cannot assume that a statement of belief in God will carry any weight. In fact, faith statements may cause more suspicion than good will. Many crimes against people and land have been committed in the name of God. Today, earth-keepers must demonstrate their faith in the way they live. That is probably the only strategy that may effectively enlist others in considering the guiding vision being here espoused.

## God's Earth a Sacred Trust

In itself, earth is not holy or sacred. The earth is God's creation; God alone is holy. God is to be worshiped, not the earth. Similarly, human beings are God's creatures and in no way divine. Certain places may be regarded as holy because God's interaction with humankind is commemorated there, but this is only a functional sacredness and not absolute. Certain people may be set aside as holy for special holy tasks, but they too have only a derived holiness. Creatures and the created can point to God's holiness, but they do not in themselves become holy. Humankind has value and life because the holy God, the Creator, so wills.

That earth is not rightly regarded as holy, however, does not mean that it is valueless or that it can be used for any purpose. God created humankind for the very important tasks of worshiping God and caring for God's land, earth. As humans till garden–earth, they are provided nourishing food and beautiful surroundings. God never intended that human beings should arrogantly presume that they could do anything they please with God's good land. Exploiting or wasting earth's resources is irresponsible and a violation of God's trust. This does not mean that every property-development project or every act that alters the environment is automatically to be judged as wrong. Rather, the trust means we must accept that the world does not ultimately belong to humankind. Humans have been given a charge to care for garden-earth, benefit from it, and pass it to the next generation in such a way that all will be able to understand and celebrate the wonder of God's gift to humankind.

The human record as earth-keepers, particularly during the past two centuries, is not good. In the name of progress and with a desire for personal or national gain, or both, all manner of destructive exploitation has been sanctioned and carried out. The incredible polluting of Eastern Europe that has come to light in recent years provides a vivid image of how much harm can be done. The industrialized nations of the West may, in some instances, be coming to a new understanding of ecological crises, but they still have a long way to go to right the wrongs already committed.

Israel, and all the other nations in the Middle East, are set under the same mandate by God to care for the land, for earth. Likewise, and perhaps even more urgently because of their size and capacity to affect the environment, the wealthiest industrialized nations—the United States, Germany, Japan, and others—are responsible to God. Humans are to care for earth! Water, air, and soil are to be shared and enjoyed, not hoarded, polluted, used wastefully, or for the advantage of one over another. God's earth may not be sacred in itself, but it is a sacred trust given into human care.

## God's Earth-keepers

The Bible's opening chapters are devoted to God, God's creating acts, and the relationship of God with the creation. A special relationship is described between God and humankind: Female and male, together created in God's image and capable of interacting with one another and God. Human-kind was created unlike all other creatures and given respon-sibility for the whole of creation. These opening chapters of Genesis are remarkable in their presentation of the impor-tance and place of humanity in God's vision.

Several things are especially important to note. The open-ing chapters of Genesis are not about Israel but about hu-mankind—the whole human family—and the larger creation to which all humans belong. Certainly, ancient Israel remem-bered the Genesis accounts as prelude to the national history, but in themselves these chapters present a wider scene, a global scene, and insist that all humankind be understood as God's creation. All humans have the same God, the only God of the universe, as their Creator, whether they acknowledge this or not. The affirmation that God, the God of the Bible, is Creator of all is fundamental.

Genesis makes another more subtle point. Human beings are made in God's image and likeness (Gen. 1:26–27). The Hebrew terminology used here is rather technical. Most often the term "image," for instance, refers to a statue or symbol of a ruler. Ancient rulers put up images of themselves as re-minders of who was in charge. As well as erecting idols of the gods they worshiped, conquerors would place their own image at the borders of a vanquished country or in the center of a captured city. Similarly, human beings as made in God's image stand as living reminders of the Ruler of all, the Cre-ator. Creation belongs to God, and God's image is planted throughout earth to remind all creatures of God's priority. Rather than suggesting ways in which human souls are like God's or reflect God's Spirit, as later Christian theology came to contend, to affirm human beings as created in God's image means that human beings have been given the responsibility of representing God in the midst of God's creation.

As already noted, however, humankind has not been given license to do anything it wills. Care of the creation is the main agenda. Protestant Christianity, by its connection with emerg-ing capitalism in the eighteenth and nineteenth centuries, came to espouse a view that the biblical inspiration to "fill the earth and subdue it" (Gen. 1:28) meant that humans could do anything they pleased with earth and earth's creatures, and great exploitation and waste resulted. Today, there is a growing awareness that the previous interpretation of God's directive was wrong. As representatives of God, humans are expected to show the same regard and care for earth as does God. The creation was "good" and brought delight to God. Humans who stand in God's image are to point to the Ruler, to the God of the Universe, to the one who loves the world so much that nothing will be allowed to destroy the relationship of creator and creature, a love that Christians believe became incarnate in Jesus of Nazareth for the sake of all.

One other comment is in order here. In the picture presented by Genesis and affirmed in other places in the Bible, all human beings are designated as earth-keepers. All stand in God's image and all carry a common charge. No chosen ones bear special responsibility or privilege. Israel was not assigned this special task. Israel's history may give testimony to God's intention and God's unwillingness to let human negligence or rebellion be the last word, but being earth-keepers is not the peculiar task of Israel. The tending of creation, the caring, loving tilling of garden-earth, is intended as the work of all humankind. The question is not whether one will be an earth-keeper. Rather, the question is whether one will be a good earth-keeper. The guiding vision assigns to all the role of earth-keepers and then provides direction on what good earth-keepers will do. Further, because all are charged as earth-keepers, we should cooperate with and form coalitions with any who have glimpsed the vision and are striving to fulfill it as good earth-keepers.

## God's Allocation of Land

Each individual and each group needs land, a part of the earth, for support and development. In the Bible, God is described as allocating land for each of the peoples of earth.

Such a notion becomes hopelessly complex if literally applied within the modern context. The point is that land is essential for humans to have a full life. People need space, a place where they can be who they are to be. Whether, following Abraham's example, the less fertile is taken instead of the more fertile is not nearly so important as that each people have their own land. In industrialized cultures, individual land ownership may be severely reduced, with personal belongings only symbolic of this basic need. Nonetheless, people continue to live in communities, ethnic and national, that express and press their desire for their own land.

The difficulty comes, obviously, when the claims of one person or group conflict with the claims of another. Within modern Israel, for instance, conflicting claims have created great tension and strife. The same is true in Bosnia, Ireland, Azerbaijan, Central America, and communities within the United States. While it is convenient to claim a God-given right to land, such a claim is invalid unless it includes the conviction that others have the same God-given right to land. The tradition of God's allotment cannot be used to settle boundary disputes. The tradition only asserts God's fundamental intention that all people have a place. This is part of the guiding vision.

Residents of modern Israel have a right to a secure land in which to live and develop their culture. Their rights are no greater than those of others, but they are real and justified. Israelis do not have a divine right to any land, however, unless it is understood that all peoples have such rights.

In trying to assist in the settlement of land disputes, the recognition of divine intention is most important. The best stance will usually be that both (or all) parties have rights and responsibilities, rather than one or the other. How can Jews and Muslims and Christians live together in one place? How can the hopes of each group be acknowledged and honored? What compromises are necessary? Possible? In the final analysis, the guiding vision insists that God has allotted earth to humankind and has given human beings the necessary intelligence to work out the details. The needs and dreams of each person and group are at stake when anyone is deprived unjustly. Good earth-keepers cannot rest until just solutions are found and implemented.

## God's Absolute Claim

The conviction that the earth is God's land necessarily implies that no individual or nation can claim absolute ownership of territory. God's land claim alone is primary and absolute. At best, humans have only secondary rights. All are living on someone else's land, God's land. Humans occupy places for shorter or longer periods of time, but they never truly own them. Humans use space wisely or stupidly, for the well-being of all or selfishly, to build up or to tear down, but they have no absolute right to their land. Earth—all of it— was created by God and belongs to God who instructs human beings to live on it responsibly and peacefully.

The absolute claim of God that overrides all other claims is difficult for many people to recognize or accept. Because many do not believe in God, they are even less willing to accept that they hold secondary rights to land. Earth-keepers seeking to follow God's guiding vision may have to risk giving up their own land claims to set an example so that others may be treated more equitably. Given human propensity toward greed and selfishness, voluntary acts of self-denial are difficult and dangerous. Nonetheless, some may have to adjust their claims in the light of God's absolute claim and the needs of others to enjoy some portion of God's land.

## Living in *Shalom*

On the basis of the guiding vision, God's intention is that all people will live in *shalom,* in peace. Milk and honey, the messianic banquet, the end of pain and suffering—all of these biblical images are part of the picture drawn to explain God's desires for the human family. Earth is sufficiently fertile and productive that all may be fed and enjoy clear water and fresh air. Garden-earth, the blue planet, has the resources. Thus far, however, proper conduct by earth-keepers has been lacking. Call it the result of sin (as Reformed Christians usually do) or obstinate stupidity (as others might prefer), humankind has chosen to ignore God's vision for the earth and has pursued much more selfish and shortsighted interests. Earth can provide, but not indefinitely. Earth-keepers are expected to live responsibly and peacefully.

What does it mean to live responsibly and peacefully? Is it impossibly difficult? Not from the biblical point of view. As Creator, God can and has set the standard: justice. In the Bible, justice is the result of people doing what they are required or expected to do on the basis of defined relationships. People who honor their commitments to one another are righteous and their acts are just. The same applies in relationship with God. If humans live righteously, they will exploit neither earth nor one another. If they make justice their aim, they will be sensitive to and supportive of the least among them, particularly the homeless and the poor (Lev. 19:9–10; Deut. 24:17–22). In the Bible, use of land is tied directly to doing justice, loving mercy, and maintaining a respectful relationship with God. Caring for the land and for one another is the standard by which land occupancy is measured.

For instance, modern Israel's treatment of those within its legal borders as well as those in the occupied territories is of great importance. Israel's military rule should certainly be judged by international standards, as would be those of any nation. Any judgment leveled at Israel should also be applied to other governments. But a degree of justice that goes beyond international standards is also expected on the basis of the biblical tradition that informs the guiding vision articulated here. Israel's military rule may indeed be more humane than many in history, as is sometimes suggested. Nonetheless, the reported abuses of Palestinians—and these are too numerous and too well documented to be dismissed—dishonor Israel. Biblical justice includes setting things right so that reconciliation may be possible. Remember, though, values drawn from religious conviction that inform judgments about national behavior must be applied equally to all—to Israel, to the Arab nations surrounding Israel, and to every other nation whose conduct is under scrutiny.

Palestinians also have a right to a secure land in which to live and develop their culture. Individual Palestinians have lost much as a result of the wars between the Arab nations and Israel. Some form of reparation is in order. The establishment of a separate Palestinian state is not viewed with favor by most Israelis, but something must be done. Though four decades late, the Palestinians in the occupied territories now acknowledge Israel's legal right to the boundaries in effect from 1948 to 1967, based on the actions of the United Nations. They do not, on the other hand, seem eager to return to being part of Jordan. How a sufficient degree of autonomy could be established while ensuring the security of both Israel and the Palestinians in the West Bank and Gaza posed an impasse for many years, but the elections of 1992 returned the Labor Party to power and provided a mandate to find a peaceful solution to this dilemma. Now, with mutual recognition by Israel and the PLO, the long and arduous task of forging this solution may at last begin.

Human-rights issues associated with land claims are not the unique problem of Israel, however. In many parts of the globe, war and exploitation are carried out under the banner of land claims. The indigenous peoples of Central America, the Muslim populations in the former Yugoslavia, and the people of Tibet are some of many who have been systematically attacked and killed over land disputes and claims. The slaughter of Native Americans in North America, the massacre of 1,800,000 Armenians by the Turks between 1894 and 1918, and Hitler's attempt to exterminate the Jews are so hideous that one would think the world would learn and turn to God's way of responsibility and peace based on justice for all. But so far, this has not happened.

Time is running out for earth-keepers. Science suggests that garden-earth may well survive, but without the humans God placed in it to care for and enjoy it. God does not desire the extinction of humankind, but humans may do it to themselves. Good earth-keepers must become messengers of *shalom* if humankind is to survive and fulfill its appointed destiny. Christians, Jews, and Muslims need to cease fighting and begin working for the good of garden-earth. If ever a time existed when ethnic or religious self-interest made sense or could be justified, that time is past. All must work together. The strong must defend the interests of the weak. Justice is the way to *shalom,* a peace that all desire and for which all have been created.

## No Easy Way

Reformed Christians believe that human beings are given freedom and responsibility; humans are not choiceless puppets, automatons programmed for unthinking, uncaring, irresponsible existence. Rather, human beings have been created with the capacity to discern and to choose better over worse. They don't always do what they are capable of doing—indeed, they often ignore or renounce their own capacities. Nonetheless, humans are not invariably bound to make the wrong choice, either.

When reflecting upon land and its significance, its availability, and its necessity, humans will always be tempted to be partisan, narrow-minded, grasping, defensive, suspicious. After all, human history offers numerous examples of land being taken by one group at the expense of another. People certainly cannot afford to forget history or be overly optimistic when assessing the likelihood of human charity. Reformed Christians know about sin and the destructiveness it brings. Humans seem to be especially vulnerable to sin when it comes to land, probably because they recognize how very important land is.

The goal and hope is to be led by the guiding vision of God's intention. God desires justice among peoples so that all may prosper in peace. Humans must continue to remind themselves and others that the earth belongs to God and only secondarily is given into the care of human beings, earth-keepers. Earth is not holy, but neither is it to be used in an exploitative, destructive fashion. Humans are expected to live in ways that bring well-being to as many beings as possible, and they should never be satisfied until all are able to live life fully in God's good land. And yes, reconciliation of Christians with Muslims and Jews, of Israelis with Arabs, of all the involved parties—that too is part of the guiding vision, the basis of hope.

## Conclusion

The guiding vision I articulate in this book is simple, yet demanding. Human beings across the centuries and in a variety of cultures have shown a deep desire for and attachment to land. Claims and counterclaims have been made to justify conquests and occupations. The need for concrete, this-world space seems essential for human communities. A genuine search for ways to deal with disputes and tension is also imperative. The responsible sharing of God-created and God-owned land is the issue.

A method of analysis is suggested here. Because I assume theological convictions, some will find the approach unsatisfactory. Reformed Christians find at least three types of information especially important for the process of forming opinions and understanding: (1) historical reality; (2) biblical accounts and imagery; and (3) theological constructs.

Historical reality is the first critical ingredient. What has actually happened? What in fact exists? Although debating how God interacts with human beings in the historical process, Reformed Christians agree that the history of humankind here on this very real planet Earth is important to God.

The second ingredient, the Bible, supplies essential data, providing a perspective by which to interpret and evaluate ongoing experience. Biblical accounts are time-conditioned, meaning that they were addressed to specific historical situations and real people in those situations. Nevertheless, the Bible offers both examples of how God and people have related and paradigms of how humans may expect God to act and how God has directed human beings to live.

Finally, theological affirmation, creedal statements, and doctrinal deductions inform Reformed Christians. What the church believes is seriously considered. The formation of theology is ongoing. This book seeks to make a contribution to that enterprise.

On the basis of reflection rooted in historical reality, biblical accounts and imagery, and theological construction related to the emergence of the modern state of Israel, I have now moved to a rather encompassing position. Concern for a particular place, Israel, and over the struggles of the people living there has led to insight about the situation and also has suggested a stance by which to approach similar issues in many parts of the world.

The guiding vision is simple, yet demanding. God has created earth and is the only legitimate land owner. God has created humankind in the divine image, thereby appointing them earth-keepers responsible for tilling and sharing garden-earth. God's intention is that humankind will enjoy and preserve the beauty and fecundity of earth for the good of all who now or in the future will inhabit God's good land. The way to the peace, *shalom*, that God intends is through justice and equity. While not always easy to accomplish, the guiding vision assures all of the appropriateness and possibility of such a peace.

Earth-keepers are given the option of following God's way or rejecting it. God's way is marked by compassion for the weak and vulnerable, regard for justice and equity, and acknowledgment of the genuine need of each person for a safe place to live and flourish. Good earth-keepers will accept the challenge to use God-given intellect and skill to develop and implement strategies for *shalom*. The adjustment of individual lifestyles as well as the analysis and transformation of human systems will be matters of concern and cooperation.

For some, the establishment of modern Israel has been proclaimed the herald of the Messianic Age. In view of biblical statements and historical reality, such claims seem extravagant. It seems better to see the creation of Israel as the result of political events that may have religious significance but not as a part of a mysterious, divine plan loaded with mystical meaning. The history of Israel dramatizes the needs of human communities for secure land while also concretely illustrating the conflicts that often surround land claims and land acquisition. Any serious consideration of the significance of Israel will eventually press on to other peoples and other land disputes, each concretely different and yet so similar.

Indeed, some have called the establishment of modern Israel a "miracle." Such a label is accurate on at least one count. The primary function of miracles in the Bible is to point past themselves to the God who is their source. The miracle of Israel does point beyond itself with a strong reminder that the world is to be understood as belonging to God. The fact of modern Israel has prompted a reconsideration of relationships between Christians, Jews, and Muslims and of God's desire that all live together. Somewhat as did ancient Israel, modern Israel, in its struggles to be what its tradition calls it to be, gives rise to renewed reflection about God's way for all humankind. Israel's failures are paralleled in many places around the globe in a variety of conflicts over land. Israel's standards, based on biblical as well as democratic ideals, challenge all to a higher way.

In examining the example of modern Israel, a wider, more inclusive vista appears, namely God's desire for all peoples and nations. And what is God's desire? A just peace in which all may live and prosper. A sharing and honoring of God's land, earth, is God's desire and the challenge placed before each earth-keeper. No one can make any of us respond, but each of us knows in our hearts that God's way is finally the only way to the security and freedom we all long to enjoy. Shall we join arms, or shall we continue to twist arms and break legs and resist common sense and common cause?

Earth-keeper, the choice is ours.

*For Further Reading*

On global land and ecology issues:

Ambler, Rex. *Global Theology*. Philadelphia: Trinity Press International, 1990.

Evans, Bernard F. and Gregory D. Cusack, eds. *Theology of the Land*. Collegeville, Minn.: Liturgical Press, 1987.

Granberg-Michaelson, Wesley. *Tending the Garden—Essays on the Gospel and the Earth*. Grand Rapids, Mich.: William B. Eerdmans Publishing, 1987.

Lilburne, Geoffrey R. *A Sense of Place: A Christian Theology of the Land*. Nashville: Abingdon Press, 1989.

May, R. H. Jr. *The Poor of the Land*. Maryknoll, N.Y.: Orbis Books, 1991.

Metz, J. B. and Edward Schillebeeckx, eds. *No Heaven Without Earth*. Philadelphia: Trinity Press, 1991.

*Restoring Creation for Ecology and Justice*. Louisville, Ky.: Office of the General Assembly, Presbyterian Church (U.S.A.), 1990.

On Palestinian justice issues:

Ateek, Naim Stifan. *Justice, and Only Justice: A Palestinian Theology of Liberation*. Maryknoll, N.Y.: Orbis Books, 1989.

Friedman, Thomas L. *From Beirut to Jerusalem*. New York: Farrar, Straus & Giroux, 1989.

Ruether, Rosemary Radford and Herman J. Ruether. *The Wrath of Jonah: The Crisis of Religious Nationalism in the Israeli-Palestinian Conflict*. San Francisco: HarperCollins, 1989.

# Group Study Guide

*First Discussion: The Preface*

1. Begin by locating and discussing the thesis. What might it mean to say that land is on loan from God? What do you think responsible use of land entails? How do you expect the Bible to be involved in this study?
2. Next, name and discuss the three primary goals set by the author. How are they related to the thesis? Identify several theological affirmations central to the author.
3. Finally, make a brief list of conclusions you believe you may anticipate on the basis of the preface. Keep your list and refer to it as you work your way through the book as a way to measure the author's success in meeting the announced goals or as a means of clarifying your own understanding of the author's intention.

*Second Discussion: Chapter 1*

1. Begin by discussing opinions of the various people. Which views surprised you or seem peculiar to you? Why are those views surprising? Strange? Do Jews and Arabs (Christians and Muslims) seem to agree on some points? Do you share the views of any one (or several) of those people?
2. Next, consider the implications of the pluralism found in Israel. What points of agreement, if any, can be found among the different points of view? How is the pluralism

in Israel like or unlike that in the United States? Discuss the similarity and difference between the nationalistic and religious claims of Jews and Arabs over the land.

3. Finally, discuss the author's statement: "Formulations based on religion have often been more hurtful than helpful. Nonetheless there is a religious, a theological dimension to the talk about land that cannot be ignored." What are some of the reasons (negative and positive) for this contention? If one does consider land from a religious or theological perspective, what are some of the dangers to which to be sensitive and careful?

An alternate strategy, depending upon the number of discussions you want to plan and the character of your group, would be to ask individuals in the group to take the parts of the people at the two gates and have a panel discussion representing these different views. You might also invite some Jews and Arabs living in your community to visit your group and share their views of land. Were you to follow this approach, you would probably fashion one or even two separate discussions around the first step.

*Third Discussion: Chapter 2*

1. Begin by discussing the importance of being historically informed before making political and theological judgments. In what ways have you experienced the accuracy of the author's contention that "theological reflection apart from historical reality can foster misunderstanding if not outright error." How is prejudice involved? Religious fanaticism? What are some of the sources of information that you can draw upon? Why are multiple witnesses or sources to be sought? How would you characterize the information you receive through the news media concerning Israel? Concerning the Arab nations? How are Jews and Muslims sometimes stereotyped?

2. Next, turn to a consideration of reactions by the group to the historical review. What came as new information? If

any interpretations of the history are different from previous reports you have read, how are they different and how might they be explained? What parts of the review, if any, were basically unknown to you prior to your reading? On the basis of your own experience or previous study, how would you enhance or correct the author's review?

3. Conclude the discussion by reflecting on the present situation as you understand it. What are some of the elements that may lead to a reassessment of the conflict over land in Israel? If you were a peace negotiator, what aspects of the history would you emphasize? How does your theology or religious perspective influence your reading of history and political decision-making?

An alternate strategy, if you wish to expand this discussion into one or two additional sessions, would be to ask several in the group to do some of the "For Further Reading" to enhance the discussion suggested in the second question above. M. E. Yapp provides an excellent review of the history of the region in this century. Thomas Friedman sheds great insight on Arab and Israeli politics, the Palestine Liberation Organization, and the difficulty that Americans have in reporting and understanding events in the Middle East. Or, if you know persons who have worked, studied, or reported the news in the Middle East, one or several might be invited to discuss their impressions with the group and respond to questions the group might pose on the basis of their reading.

## Fourth Discussion: Chapter 3

1. Begin with a discussion of why and how the Bible is viewed by the author. Why is the Bible important? What are the Bible's limitations? How does the Bible help us in the consideration of current issues? Or does it? In what ways do you think you agree or disagree with the author?

2. Discuss the ways in which the Bible deals with land. Which theme was most familiar? What surprised you, came as

new information, or intrigued you about the biblical material? What are some of the ways the Old Testament and the New Testament agree or disagree about the issue of land?

3. Conclude the discussion with a consideration of the themes of human responsibility for and divine ownership of land. How pervasive is the divine requirement of human responsibility and how is this related to land? How is God's ownership of the land (and all the earth) expressed? Why is the theme "A New Heaven and a New Earth" especially important in this discussion?

An alternate strategy would be to assign group members to study particular sections of the chapter in detail, looking up the biblical passages cited and then reporting to the group. By doing this, you could begin with the first question and part of the second one, then expand the reflection described in Step 2 into one or two more discussions. Further, you might have an additional discussion in which group members report on some of the books suggested in "For Further Reading" to see how they enhance or contradict the author's presentation of the biblical material on land.

### Fifth Discussion: Chapter 4

1. Begin by considering the goal of the chapter, namely the reformulation of "a number of theological statements often heard in discussions about modern Israel and land." What historical information is used in defending or suggesting such reformulation? How does the Bible enter in? What place has God's Spirit? Can there be, as the author says, "new understandings" that replace views once considered to be true? What examples can you think of from science, church practices, or other areas of life?

2. Next, outline the seven questions presented in the chapter. Which of these theological reformulations most surprised you? Why? How has the fulfillment of prophecy worked in some theological systems and how does the author

approach this biblical idea? What does the author believe
it is appropriate to say theologically about Israel? Do you
agree or disagree? How does your theology influence you
on these issues?

3. Conclude by asking the group to consider the author's
affirmation near the end of the chapter: "Reformed Christians contend that God's promises are sure, God's commitments are real, and God's intentions for justice and peace
remain unqualified." What does this statement mean to
you in light of the preceding discussion? Would you affirm
the same thing? Why? Why not?

   An alternate strategy would be to have members of the
group read some of the material in "For Further Reading"
and then prepare reports on dispensationalism, fundamen-
talism, and Jewish-Christian relationships. One to three
sessions could be devoted to this material and used to sup-
plement the questions posed in the first and second steps.

*Sixth Discussion: Chapter 5*

1. Begin by discussing the need for a "guiding vision." Why is
a vision important? What are some characteristics of the
vision of which the author writes? How have such guiding
concepts or life ambitions worked in your experience?
What are the limits of such dreams?

2. Next, discuss the content of the guiding vision presented by
the author. What is central? How are God, earth, and human beings related? What are some of the implications of
viewing earth as a sacred trust? How is the distribution of
land to be viewed in light of God's absolute claim? What
does it mean for earth-keepers to live in *shalom*?

3. Conclude by asking the group to reread and react to the
concluding paragraph of the chapter. Has the author made
his case? Is it legitimate to contend that: "A sharing and
honoring of God's land, earth, is God's desire and the challenge placed before each earth-keeper"? If so, what is to be
done?

An alternate strategy might be to devote several sessions to the issues posed in the second step. Ecological implications could be explicitly developed in response to questions about the responsibility of earth-keepers for the earth. Human rights issues could be explained more fully in connection with the section on living in *shalom*. Finally, specific projects might be adopted which would put into action the guiding vision developed by the author.